FLOURISHING
— ACROSS —
CULTURES

A STEP-BY-STEP GUIDE
FROM DISCERNING TO RETURNING

ISBN: 979-8-9925809-0-7 (Paperback)
ISBN: 979-8-9925809-1-4 (E-book)

For bulk purchase, contact: David Harakal at DHarakalAuthor@gmail.com.

Because of the dynamic nature of the Internet, web addresses or links contained in this book may have been changed since publication and may no longer be valid. The content of this book and all expressed opinions are those of the author and do not reflect the publisher or the publishing team. The author is solely responsible for all content included herein.

Unless otherwise indicated, all Scripture quotations are taken from *The ESV® Bible (The Holy Bible, English Standard Version®)*, copyright © 2001 by Crossway, a publishing ministry of Good News Publishers. Used by permission. All rights reserved.

Scripture quotations marked KJV are taken from the *King James Version*. Public domain.

Library of Congress Control Number: 2025903157
Cover design by M. Naeem
Interior design by Marigold02k via Fiverr
Proofread by Jessie Raymond

FIRST EDITION

FLOURISHING
— ACROSS —
CULTURES

A STEP-BY-STEP GUIDE
FROM DISCERNING TO RETURNING

DAVID HARAKAL

Our tenure on the field has not been long, but God has provided us an unusual breadth of experiences through our role in member care.

We did not plan for this life. Our Father had it planned from the beginning.

I am most thankful to my wife, Suzanne. We suffered and found joy together on this journey.

As I wrote this book, many people shared thoughts, advice, corrections, and ideas. Given the nature of our work, I cannot share their names. You know who you are, and I thank you.

TABLE OF CONTENTS

PREFACE

My wife and I have lived in three different cross-cultural settings. Though continents and decades apart, and our reasons for leaving completely different, the similarity in cultural shifts surprised me.

We met in Oxford, England on a study-abroad program during college, then settled into American suburbia and started our family. Seven years into our marriage, our first international transition was for a corporate growth assignment in England. Packers showed up at our home, packed everything into a twenty-foot container, and unloaded it on the other side of the ocean. We landed with a car, a housekeeper, a gardener, and a bank account with money in it.

Twenty-four years later, we moved in eight suitcases to a tumultuous third-world nation.

Our first cross-cultural move included our young children.

This time we left grown, married children.

In 1996, we moved to a country whose language we mistakenly thought was virtually the same as ours (Texas to England).

In 2020, we landed in a country where we would not master the local language (Arabic) if we studied for the rest of our lives.

God provided us with a crash course in cross-cultural living. During our relatively short tenure, we experienced political unrest, financial collapse, deaths of family members, births of grandchildren, international moves between unfamiliar countries, unplanned relocation, frequent leadership changes, misaligned expectations, team changes, societal discord, riots, war, and many goodbyes.

My writing style is dogmatic to be succinct and challenge thought. Others might offer a range of choices to answer every question. For those already overwhelmed, or headed in that direction (as I was), blunt and to-the-point is more helpful. In times of decision fatigue, you need: "Go here. Do this. Buy that." You can revisit your decisions when you have the mental capacity to do so—when you are out of the cross-cultural fog.

The Back Story

I love Jesus. That love pervades this book, but it is rarely prevalent. My wife and I would not have burned the ships[1] and moved to a country vastly out of our comfort zone if we did not love our Lord more than our lives.

This is not the life we planned. I bought the lie that the comforts we enjoyed through successful jobs and robust incomes meant we would comfortably participate in the great commission as financial supporters, providing for those who were called to leave the ease of home to go somewhere foreign and uncomfortable to expand God's kingdom. However, our children and their spouses planned to move onto the battlefield. To remain near to them, without giving up our life of comfort, we considered opening a "care center" somewhere pleasant in Western Europe, palatable to our life of ease.

Mann tracht, un Gott lacht is an old Yiddish adage translated, "Man plans, and God laughs." Our children and grandchildren are in our passport country, and we live in a challenging environment where we will never fully integrate. I can imagine our God smiling, knowing his plans for our good and his glory, to grow and sanctify us as we help those he has called to the front lines in the battle for souls. We have seen God

---

[1] A reference to the historically inaccurate but philosophically true portrayal of Hernán Cortés's landing in Mexico in 1519, where his ships were scuttled for building materials and to make it impossible for his troops to evacuate when things became difficult. (One was kept intact to send sought-after riches to the King of Spain.) So, while not literally burned, the troops were "all in" with no effective means of retreat. (Glenn Stanton, "FactChecker: Burning Your Ships for Jesus," thegospelcoalition.org, The Gospel Coalition, March 13, 2013, https://www.thegospelcoalition. org/article/ factchecker-burning-your-ships-for-Jesus/.)

use us in myriad ways during our time on the field, and one purpose is to create this resource for those who come after us.

In 2020, I left my career in corporate America after my wife left her elementary teaching position. We sold our home of twenty-seven years and moved away from our recently married children to the Middle East/North Africa region. Our overseas tenure has not been long, but we have learned from those in dozens of organizations who have lived cross-culturally for months to decades.

I believed that a profit-oriented career in business disqualified me for mission. Apparently not! Missions need structures to help individuals and organizations define and reach goals. All teams, companies, sending fellowships, NGOs, etc., require leadership, management, and clear operating principles. The worlds of business and mission are not wholly dissimilar. In the missions field, we want to increase our share of the world faith market by sharing truths that God will use to lead people to an eternal heavenly future, while for-profit businesses desire an increasing share of a product market and its profits. We all sell something. The missionary's offering—salvation for the lost soul through the death and resurrection of Jesus—is of the greatest value. If you are in the mission field and disagree, you are in the wrong line of work!

The experience God has given me in my decades of restructuring corporate portfolios and integrating companies acquired through acquisition, serving as a deacon and an elder in a large American church, leading in the Boy Scouts of America (now Scouting America), and serving in our children's school, plus thirty-five years of marriage and raising two children, prepared me for the work He has called me to do.

We describe our primary job as "team parents." Those on the field early in their lives (single, young couples, young families) benefit from people in our life phase who are not their bosses nor their assigned member-care representatives—but who provide a listening ear, someone to translate for their parents, and come alongside them in their marriage and parenting struggles, sometimes complicated by life on the field, but just as often challenging because marriage and parenting are hard for broken people in a fallen world.

To use a military analogy, we are not front-line soldiers. But the front-line soldier will die without medics and supply line managers. We are like the field hospital that patches the small wounds to prevent them from becoming large wounds, or to stabilize someone for a move or until long-term care is unavailable.

God uses the gifts and experiences he has given us to do his work in ways we had never planned—or imagined.

David Harakal
October 2024

INTRODUCTION

Whatever you do, work heartily, as for the Lord and not for men …
—Colossians 3:23

Never be afraid to trust an unknown future to a known God.
—Corrie Ten Boom

Moving to a new culture can be daunting—exciting, but daunting.

Settling into a new country may be unsettling.

Making your home in a place that may never accept you can be disheartening.

As a cross-cultural worker called God to serve God in full-time ministry, your calling is holy. For the follower of Jesus, his call to a new country to work for a commercial enterprise, a government, or a non-governmental organization (NGO), is a call to further his kingdom.

John Piper said, "God is most glorified in us when we are most satisfied in him." Those around you need to see you at your most satisfied. They need to see you flourish.

But so much gets in the way! Elements of a foreign culture may be confusing, complicated, and frustrating. They may seem to preclude you from the work you were sent to do. The mundane tasks required by your company, sending organization, or supporters can be a distraction.

I want to guide you out of the fog, to demystify the cross-cultural journey.

During our transitions, we could not find what we needed—a concise resource that covers every step from considering leaving to returning to one's passport country. We were offered books and podcasts and blogs and websites and consultants. Most of them were excellent, but the flood of words on excessive pages and conference calls exacerbated our sense of overload. We needed this to help us navigate our way.

This is your "Cliffs Notes" for discerning your call or evaluating an international assignment to returning from the field after a few years or several decades. Find succinct, tried-and-true recommendations for healthy single and married life, parenting and leading, navigating contracts and reporting—all complicated by life in a culture not your own.

My hope is to provide you with a tool to visit time and again when you need clarity for the next phase in your journey or as your work or personal life changes. When the future looks intimidating, the bullet points and bold keywords will help you make the right next step. I want to strip away the noise and confusion crowding your thoughts so you can focus on Jesus and the work he has sent you to do.

This Book Is Different

Breadth plus brevity differentiates this book from others. Checklists and bullet points replace most pages of prose for easy consumption, with keywords and phrases in bold for easy navigation. My goal is to provide succinct advice for what to do, consider, or expect, and when, to help alleviate your fear, uncertainty, and doubt. This book has a few anecdotes. Each chapter has recommendations that delve more deeply into the topic.

As a cross-cultural ministry worker, I write particularly to the Christian pursuing Christ's call to international work. As a former study-abroad student and Fortune 500 expatriate, I know the broad benefit of the recommendations I offer.

The member care my wife and I provide gives me insights well beyond my own experiences. My network provided me with dozens of reviewers with varied experiences, tenures on the field, geographical locations, life phases, sending organizations, and nature of work (ministry workers, NGO employees, UN and employees of different countries' embassies).

Learn from others' mistakes—then go make new ones.

You, your sending fellowship or organization, or receiving team may not agree with my suggestions. When we started this work, I did not agree with much of what I propose here. One of the most important skills to carry with you into a new culture is your ability to learn and adapt. I hope you will evaluate the merits or the recommendations with which you may not initially agree.

I focus on the nuts and bolts, the "how's" more than the "whys," the "just tell me what I need to do." If you want theological reasons for mission (which I believe or I would not be so far from home!), I recommend Wayne Grudem's *Systematic Theology*, John Piper's *Let the Nations Be Glad*, and Thomas Hale's *On Being a Missionary* (Abridged).

Though my desire is brevity, you will find some repetition, as I expect most readers to read only the chapter most pressing for them at the time.

Definitions, Errors, or Suggestions

If you discover errors or omissions, or you have suggestions about any facet of this resource, please contact me at DHarakalAuthor@gmail.com.

Disclaimer

My views and opinions are my own and may or may not align with any entity with which I am now or have been affiliated. They may also not align with your sending agency, fellowship, or company.

I designed this book to be used with team or organization field manuals and policies, not to contradict them. My goal is to give you a bird's-eye view to see how all the pieces fit together, cover topics which manuals may not, and fill in gaps for those without such resources.

This book is based on my own successes and failures, what I have seen work well or not for others, and the advice of cross-cultural workers I know and trust.

PART ONE

YOUR JOURNEY FROM DISCERNING TO RETURNING

CHAPTER ONE

FLOURISHING

*The thief comes only to steal and kill and destroy. I came
that they may have life and have it abundantly.*

—John 10:10

The future is as bright as the promises of God.

—William Carey

Flourishing. We are supposed to do it, or strive towards it, but what is it?

From *merriam-webster.com/dictionary*: Flourish (ˈflə-rish), intransitive verb

1.   to grow luxuriantly : thrive
2a.   to achieve success : prosper
2b.   to be in a state of activity or production
2c.   to reach a height of development or influence
3.   to make bold and sweeping gestures

Synonyms: burgeon, bourgeon, prosper, thrive

I avoided the more often used verb **"thrive"** because, in addition to being hijacked by TikTok in 2024, the word is **often overused and misunderstood** to mean:

- The ultimate **source of happiness and contentment** ("You just need to learn to thrive in your context," implying one "just" needs to try harder to make oneself happy; that this is a realistic goal without dependence on Christ alone for contentment.)
- A **reason for leaving** ("I/we cannot thrive here," used to over-spiritualize inconveniences and missed comforts.)
- A **shame-burdened challenge** ("If you just ..., you will thrive," without providing a robust theology of suffering along with practical tools to navigate a new culture.)

Pursuit of Biblically defined flourishing is the mark of a mature believer. John 10:10 promises an abundant life. I paraphrase Psalm 37:4: God promises to give you the desires of your heart, predicated on your first delighting in him.

I define "flourishing" as being happy, healthy, and holy, or moving in that direction. God often uses the absence of one or more of those elements to remind us of our need for our savior, to remind the believer what they believe, to sanctify us.

To help you flourish, minimize that which unnecessarily complicates life, especially in a new context. Notice the word "unnecessarily"—not all of your challenges are unnecessary or unavoidable, but too often people make situations more difficult than they need to be.

Tips to Help You Flourish

Pray.
- A quote I heard growing up that I cannot attribute is, "The best form of spiritual exercise is to touch the floor regularly with your knees."
- Philippians 4:6-8 reminds us to take everything to the Lord in prayer, to open the door to the peace only he can offer.

Decide to be content.
- 1 Thessalonians 5:16-18 begins with "Rejoice always," followed by praying continually and being thankful in all things.

- o This implies that contentment is more of a decision than a feeling.
- You may not choose what happens to you, but you have complete control over how you respond.
- **Reject a victim mentality.**
  - o Terrible things happen in our fallen world, but they cannot drive your identity.

Embrace change and uncertainty.

- Life in an unfamiliar country can be challenging—language, culture, food, customs, norms are all different.
- Frequent change is a common experience in cross-cultural work.
- Remember the Jewish proverb, "Man plans, and God laughs."
  - o His ways are not our ways and are harder than we might prefer sometimes.
- **Learn.**
  - o Your "learner attitude" in all situations will help reduce frustration and bitterness.
- **Keep an open mind.**
  - o Your role on a team, your plans, and your expectations may change during every step of your process.
  - o Rigid plans and timelines are a recipe for discontentment.
- **Be patient.**
  - o You will adapt.

Respond promptly.

- When someone reaches out to you, respond as soon as you can—it doesn't have to be a long response.
- **If someone asks you a question, answer it!**
- Your response can be a date for a date (e.g., I will answer more fully by <date>).
- Some have found it helpful to **set aside time each day to reply** to communications to keep emails and messages from invading working time.

- Responsiveness will help you maintain short accounts and avoid frustrating those who want to help you.

Set reasonable expectations.
- Talk to others in your context.
- In many countries, buying groceries or paying a utility bill may be a reasonable expectation for a day's accomplishment!

Laugh easily and often—do not take yourself too seriously.
- When you commit some cultural *faux pax* or use the wrong word, find the humor in it.
- Anecdote: I used the wrong word and told the security person at the airport that I had a suitcase full of parks instead of gifts.
  - He laughed instead of inspecting my bag.

Recognize that **your ministry** is also **your job**—in addition to **your calling.**
- Create a reasonable work-life balance.
- You have a **boss** and may have **targets or quotas** to meet.
- Legal and spiritual accountability may be uncomfortable at times.
- **Required tasks are not spiritual attacks** just because you perceive them as tangential to the work you feel called to do.
  - Every job has elements that you will not like, are not ideal, or are unpleasant.
  - You probably need to **claim expenses, file reports,** or **complete required training** that you would prefer to avoid.
  - To flourish, **complete necessary tasks promptly and without grumbling.**

Disclaimer

My views and opinions are my own and may or may not align with any entity with which I am now or have been affiliated. They may also not align with your sending agency, fellowship, or company.

—————————————————————— **Notes** ——————————————————————

Notes

CHAPTER TWO

DISCERNING

And how are they to preach unless they are sent? As it is written, "How
beautiful are the feet of those who preach the good news!"

—Romans 10:15

The history of missions is the history of answered prayer.
It is the key to the whole mission problem.
All human means are secondary.

—Samuel Marinus Zwemer

The mission field is not a place for the new believer. One new to faith may well be filled with love for our Lord and zeal to serve him, even in a remote context. Praise God! If this is you, serve him faithfully in your local context first. As your faith is tested and matures, begin your discernment process regarding cross-cultural ministry. The disciples spent nearly three years with Jesus before "he sent them out to proclaim the kingdom of God and to heal." (Luke 9:2)

Time spent discerning can be nerve-wracking, made worse if you attempt it on your own. If your primary focus is the first half of Psalm 37:4, "Delight yourself in the Lord," and you make time to listen to him over myriad other voices of friends, family, church, and company, you will grow closer to him and experience the second half of the Psalm, "... and he will give you the desires of your heart."

You need wisdom—**do not discern alone!** Include your sending fellowship, family who understands cross-cultural work, a mobilizer if you have one—those closest to you who know you best and will speak to you freely and honestly. If married, do this together and separately—you are called as individuals and a couple.

Slow down. Beware of getting caught up in the "goer torrent," where you jumped into a fast-moving river in your passion to serve the Lord and it is now moving you through the process so quickly you do not have time to listen to God or those close to you. Find a quiet pool where you can slow down and reconnect with the Lord to ensure you are still on the path he has for you.

Those moving to the field love Matthew 19:29: "And everyone who has left houses or brothers or sisters or father or mother or children or lands, for my name's sake, will receive a hundredfold and will inherit eternal life." Be careful not to focus more on the "receive" than "for my name's sake." Are you ready to leave for his name's sake alone, if you lost everything else?

Guiding Principles

- Listen to God, the counsel of Scripture, your church leaders and mentors, and your faith community (small group, counselor, *et cetera*). You need people who know your blind spots.
- Seek professional medical opinions. You must be physically and psychologically healthy enough to go.
- Couples and families with teenagers all need to agree to the calling—the struggle of cross-cultural living will affect you all.

Before your Next Steps

In your time with the Lord, with the counsel of those close to you and your worship fellowship, you decide you are ready to take your next steps.

Before you continue, you must be able to answer "Yes" to these questions, without reservations.

Are you **content?**
- You are not running away from something.
- If you are **unhappy in your home country**, and desire cross-cultural service to provide you joy and fulfillment, stop now.
    - **Make peace** with those contributing to your unrest.
    - Seek additional counsel.
- Life in a third culture often aggravates unhappiness.
    - Read Matthew 5:23-26.

Is your **prayer life regular and robust?**
- If you have studied missions, trained, learned the right tools to share the gospel, and practiced them in your home context, but do not connect with the Lord often, **develop regular prayer rhythms first.**
- You cannot expand the kingdom of God through your tenacity, endurance, or cleverness alone (though these help).
- **Unless the Holy Spirit prepares the way, you will fail before you start.**
- Develop an attitude of **"ready, willing, and unable."**
    - Only God can change a human heart.

Is your **theology solid?**
- Too many on the field have a **beautiful vision** for their work or their team, a **huge heart** for the lost, **but a shallow theology**.
- A shallow theological foundation will catch up to you and you will be unprepared for the challenges of discipleship.
    - Jesus calls us to make disciples in Matthew 28:19, not just share testimony or build churches.
- Are you prepared to address questions or statements like:
    - "Why does God allow suffering in the world?"
    - "I believe Jesus is a good way, but not the only way."
    - "How can you be sure the Bible is true?"
    - "It is not fair that evil people can go to heaven."

- If not, **stop** and invest another year or two to study systematic theology (I recommend Grudem's book referenced below), the role of suffering, the character of God, the lives of missionaries and movements, and other topics recommended by your sending fellowship or organization.
- **Seminary** may or may not be right for you. Most work I have seen in the field does not require a seminary degree.

Have you been **approved?**
- Approval by your sending organization, company, or fellowship should be a prerequisite for moving to the next steps.
- Follow the direction of **your fellowship's leaders.**
- Anecdote: As an elder, I counseled headstrong people who joined a team contrary to our guidance, and it ended very poorly for them—an avoidable mistake.
  - Pride really does go before a fall.
- You may be approved to proceed, but have not decided on the specific team or location, which is often finalized during the planning phase, and should also require approval.

Reasons to Wait

- Your sending fellowship, organization, or company **asks you to wait.**
  - Find out why.
- You are **engaged or married for less than one year.**
  - The first year of marriage has enough challenges.
  - Develop a marriage mentoring relationship with a couple at least one life phase ahead of you.
- **Your marriage is not healthy.**
  - If it is not when you depart, it is likely to deteriorate under the pressures of an unfamiliar new context.
- Your **first child is under one year** of age.
  - A child's first year has enough of its own challenges.

- ○ Develop a parenting mentoring relationship with a couple whose children are at least a life phase ahead of you.
- Your **older child is not well disciplined.**
  - ○ Develop an effective discipline model.
  - ○ Both spouses must agree to the philosophy and implementation.
  - ○ Develop a parenting mentorship.
  - ○ See the "Parenting" chapter for further information and additional resources.

Encouragement

As you seek to discover how God might use you in cross-cultural ministry, know that He has plans for you. Your goal is not what you *should* do, which would be a heavy burden. Rather, watch and listen for the plan God made for you before the world was made, to learn what you get to do—how you can join him in his work. The work you think you will do pales in comparison to what he will do in you and through you. He loves you more than what he has called you to do. Even in this stage, remember that his yoke is light.

> *And this gospel of the kingdom will be proclaimed throughout the whole world as a testimony to all nations, and then the end will come.*
>
> —Matthew 24:14

> *Decision making is easy when your values are clear.*
>
> —Roy Disney

Sample Prayer

Lord, I want to serve you and am willing to go where you ask me. So many people have an opinion. Please open my ears to those through whom you speak and deaden them to those not aligned with your plans.

If this is not the time for me to go, please prepare my heart to stay and do your work here. I need my identity to be in you alone. Please direct my steps.

Disclaimer

My views and opinions are my own and may or may not align with any entity with which I am now or have been affiliated. They may also not align with your sending agency, fellowship, or company. (Note: This disclaimer is repeated at the end of every chapter and appendix because I do not expect everyone to read every chapter.)

Additional Resources

Coleman, Robert E., *The Master Plan for Evangelism*

Frazier, David, *Mission Smart*

Grudem, Wayne, *Systematic Theology*

Hale, Thomas, *On Being a Missionary (Abridged)*

McNabb, Dr. Bob, *Spiritual Multiplication in the Real World*

Piper, John, *Let the Nations Be Glad!*

Reid, Alvin L. and Malcolm McDow, et al., *Firefall 2.0*

Ripken, Nik, *Insanity of God*

Shaw, Joey, *All Authority*

Winter, Ralph D. and Steven C. Hawthorne, *Perspectives on the World Christian Movement*

Notes

Notes

CHAPTER THREE

PREPARING

Without counsel plans fail, but with many advisers they succeed.

—Proverbs 15:22

He is no fool who gives what he cannot keep to gain what he cannot lose.

—Jim Elliot

Your fellowship has approved your desire to move overseas, you receive an offer from an NGO, or your corporate transfer request is approved. You book your tickets now, right? No! From this point, it can be months to years before you move.

You might need a visa, your role may require additional training pre-departure, or you may need to raise financial support. Work towards a date to leave, but keep this date open in your mind to avoid frustration. You will arrive when you need to be there.

During this phase, beware of getting caught up in the flow. So much will happen in rapid succession that you may miss signals to wait or change course. Take time to stop and listen to remain aligned with the plans our Father in heaven has for you.

— Guiding Principles —

- Vision trip: You need to keep yourself physically, spiritually, and emotionally healthy in your new context. Do not overlook or underestimate these needs. Will you be able to maintain your health rhythms?
- Team: Discuss the team dynamics with those close to you—these may be the only people with whom you have a relationship. Test your chemistry with the team, as dysfunctional or oppositional team dynamics are a leading cause for people who leave the field unplanned. Vision and passion will not overcome poor chemistry.
- Support: You must do your part to raise support, but recognize this is God's final go/no-go answer for you. Do not depart until fully supported and with pledges met (e.g., a promise will not pay your expenses).
- Self-care: Build your self-care network relationships in your current context well before departing. These relationships need to be developed and deepening before you go.

— Complete Pre-Field Training —

Pre-field training programs range from a few months to a few years.

- There are many offered with similar curricula.
- If the course you select does not include them, add:
    - **language preparation**, which prepares you to study a new language,
    - **cultural transition,** which trains you to adapt to a new culture.

— Team Selection —

Your team will have a significant influence over your ability to flourish, so invest the time to find the right fit.

You need a team.

- "Lone wolves" rarely succeed.
  - Being on your own (individually, as a married couple, or as a family) opens the door to avoidable loneliness and preventable spiritual decline.
- **Do not select a team for the leader** alone.
  - **Leaders come and go** with unfortunate regularity.
  - You need to **believe in the vision** and connect with other team members.
- **Trust your sending fellowship or faith community** to help you determine the right team for you.
- **Your team's theology must align** with your own and that of your sending fellowship.
  - Teams without a common theology often disintegrate with misunderstandings and hard feelings.
  - Review your church's Statement of Faith with your team and discuss any points of disagreement with the team leader and your church's leadership.
- **Ensure team and personal goals align.**
  - Discuss your goals and expectations with the team leader.
  - For example, if you want to pursue making disciples but join a church planting team, the disconnect could lead to frustration.
  - In this example, if you want to join for support and accountability as you learn language and culture and build your network, will they accommodate your different goals?
    - If so, ensure the Memorandum of Understanding (MOU) reflects your mutual expectations.
- The **theology of other teams** in your region, with whom your team partners, might differ on **secondary issues** and still result in a successful partnership.
  - Discuss your concerns with your team leader and sending fellowship.

- ○ In the field, teams benefit from each other's specialty (food distribution vs. discipleship vs. building a school, etc.).
- ○ Differences on secondary issues (infant vs. adult baptism, day of worship, music or not during the service) will rarely create substantial conflicts with partnering teams.

Carefully review your team's MOU or your contract.
- **Disregard verbal agreements or exceptions.**
  - ○ If they are not documented in the MOU, expect them not to happen.
- What is the **decision-making** structure?
  - ○ Does your sending fellowship and/or agency agree?
- Review the "Contracting" chapter for additional elements.

Treat your **initial commitment** as field training.
- Meet with your team leader(s) plus your sending organization and/or fellowship to assess your fit and potential for longevity.
- If your potential for future flourishing is low, either move to a new context or return to your prior home.
  - ○ People too often stay in a role because they cannot determine how to exit.
  - ○ Use this assessment time as your stay/go decision point.

Vision Trip

Take a vision trip before you commit to a team. Experience on the ground is much different from a video call. Your visit should last at least a week, though two would be better.

Talk to each team member, not just leaders.
- How do team members and team leaders hold each other accountable for personal holiness?
- Look for evidence of **empowered team members.**

- A leader unwilling to share leadership and delegate authority is on a path to **burnout**, and burn the team in the process.
- **Ask detailed, awkward questions.**
  - Cagey answers or uncomfortable deferrals are cause for concern.
  - Do the answers you receive align with what is written in the team's MOU?
    - If not, ask why and do not sign the MOU until it is updated.
- **Do you "click" with the team?**
  - **Team dynamics** are historically the primary reason for people leaving the field prior to their planned departure, from narcissistic leadership to a simple lack of chemistry.
  - Pray for clarity and direction.
    - It can be easy to overlook a poor interpersonal fit because you love the team's vision or exciting new context.

Spend a "day in the life."
- Participate in the team's normal rhythms.
- **Attend a language lesson**. Visit the stores, shops, or fields where you will buy food.
  - Help prepare a meal and clean up.
- Does the weekly schedule reflect the team's stated values and vision from the MOU?
  - Teams typically say they value time with the Lord, sharing, language, then admin, in that order. Do their hours during the week reflect that?
  - Note that it is normal for language learning to consume a "misaligned" share during the first several months to prepare you for future success.

Spend social time with team members' friends outside the team.
- If the team is established in a region with other expats, but no one has friends outside the team, this is **a concern**.
  - This may result from a **calendar too full** to develop friendships, which is not sustainable.

- o Or the **team is insular**, which limits the opportunity to work with other teams.
- Social time outside the team will also help you discern fit with the wider community.

What are options for church participation?
- Is there a **local church** with theology that aligns with your sending fellowship?
  - o Do team members attend? If not, why not?
  - o A team that is your work, your social life, and your worship is rarely sustainable long term.
- Are there house churches with other teams?

— Topics Specific to Life Phase —

Singles
- Are there other singles on the team or in nearby teams?
  - o If you are the only single on a team of married couples and families, you may find it particularly lonely.
  - o Discuss any special considerations for singleness in a team's context.
  - o For example, in a male-dominant conservative society, a single woman may need to be "adopted" as a daughter or sister to help navigate parts of life like police station visits for residency or even going to a mall.
- Understand the **dating policy**.

Couples
- Does the team support and do other couples practice regular date nights?

Parents
- Are there other families with children?
  - o What school options are available? Which do team members choose?
  - o Who babysits and how often?

Your vision trip was a raging success. Most are. **Do not dismiss concerns.** Seek counsel from leaders in your organization or sending fellowship plus other believers close to you.

You think you are ready to go? How will you pay for it?

Different funding models include employment, starting a business, employment by an NGO or other non-profit, or raising your own support. For any sending model, build a prayer support team.

Raising Support

This section is for those who will raise their own support through individuals and organizations.

Do your part.
- David advised his son in Chronicles 28:20, "Be strong and courageous, and do the work."
  - This was one of our "go-to" verses during our time pursuing supporters.
- Develop a **clear, concise presentation** and a plan to contact potential partners.
- Anecdote: We asked God every Sunday night for ten names, and that was who we called that week.
  - This approach reminded us **it is the Lord who provides.**
  - Your organization may have a different model.

Plan to be disappointed—and pleasantly surprised!
- Raising support is a **sanctifying process.**
- An unexpected "No" can be discouraging.
- If God wants you somewhere, he will get you there—in his timing and in his way.

Pray before every interaction.
- Ask people to **commit to pray before you ask them to pay.**
  - Prayer opens the door for God to work.

- Support is one way that **God can affirm your call or negate it, to open a door or close it.**

Set a **realistic budget.**
- Do not pick the lowest target unless you want to make your transition more difficult.
- Raise enough for a **sustainable lifestyle**—neither extravagant nor impoverished.
- Raise enough to create a savings buffer for unexpected expenses.

Do not leave until you are fully funded.
- Raising support when you are new to the field adds unnecessary stress, leading to burnout.
- Many who leave underfunded return before they had planned.
  - They tend to return disillusioned, and still underfunded.

Build Your Self-Care Network

You are responsible for your care.
- See the "Self-Care" chapter and the "Self-Care Checklist" in the appendix for a full discussion.

Develop your "advocacy team," or "A-Team."
- This is a small team of six to twelve people with whom you can share all of your needs, concerns, and challenges.
- **Exclude family members.**
  - There may be times when you need prayer for something with which your family could not cope.
- This small team should also **help with your needs** during furlough/home assignment.

Establish mentors.
- **Personal mentor**

- Choose a person at least a life phase ahead of you who understands you.
- **Marriage mentors**
  - Choose a couple in a life phase ahead of you who will contact you regularly (ideally, at least monthly).
- **Parenting mentors**
  - Choose a couple in a life phase or two ahead of you who will contact you regularly (ideally at least monthly).
- **Leadership mentor**
  - If you lead a team or want to in the future.

Clarify your **sending fellowship's relationship.**
- How often will they expect to hear from you?
- Who is your contact (general email addresses do not work)?
  - You need a **specific person** and their individual contact information.
  - Ask for commitment to **read your newsletter** and **pray for you.**
- Who has **decision-making authority** for you?
  - You may want to be your own authority, but this tends not to end well.
- What events will **require discussion, permission, or notification?**
  - Examples might include team change, changing housing, dating/ marriage, or leaving the field.
- How will they help you with planned or emergency home leave?
- Add these names to your "Self-Care Checklist" (see appendix).
- Make sure these are documented.

Legal and Financial[2]

Get your life in order. You need the following:
- **Durable power of attorney** with access to financial accounts, safe deposit boxes, and storage units

---

[2] *Note: I am neither an attorney nor a financial planner. It is best to consult with both.

- A **will** and, if you have children, a **trust and legal guardian(s)**
- **Primary and secondary beneficiaries** on all financial accounts
- A brightly colored **folder for paperwork** is helpful.
    - Print out visas, etc., even if they are online, in case there is a problem with your phone.
    - **Some countries require paper copies**, but may not note this on their websites.
- If you do not **have a credit card**, find one you can get to establish a credit pattern.
    - Purchase things on it and pay it off every month to help get a travel card later.

— *Prepare for your Financial Future* —

Pay off consumer debt before you depart.
- The added stress of making consumer debt payments while trying to serve cross-culturally may unexpectedly shorten your tenure on the field.
- Some organizations will pay off your debt to do specific work in the field.

Contribute to a retirement plan.
- Too often someone retires from a life of service in the mission field with no financial plan.
    - Do not let this happen to you.
- Many sending organizations offer different retirement plans.
- If yours does not, find a financial planner and discuss your options.
    - If you raise your own support, raise enough to contribute to retirement.

Home ownership
- **If you own a home** in a market where you can rent or lease it through a short-term, mid-term, or long-term rental, **keep it!**
    - Real estate has historically been a solid long-term investment, as long as you are not over-extended.

- ○ Caveat: only keep your home **if you can rent it and at least break even** based on conservative estimates. (Do not assume you will rent it every weekend at peak prices.)
- Find a **reliable, trustworthy property manager** with a good track record and references.
  - ○ Expect to **pay competitive rates** for quality management.
  - ○ Your old college roommate who is looking for a way to make some money on the side and wants to "try it out" with your house is not your best candidate.
  - ○ Though well-meaning, someone on your support network who wants to do you a favor is also not a good choice.
- You **may make money** on your property, which will help buffer times when your support dips.
- If there is a high probability that **you will not break even**, sell.
  - ○ The **added stress of financial need** caused by an expensive home will distract you from the reason you moved.
- Every situation is different.
  - ○ Review your plans for your home with a qualified financial planner and/or accountant.

Start

Develop your **newsletter framework** and start your discipline of **sending your newsletter regularly**.

- See the "Writing Newsletters" chapter in Part Two for additional details.
- Ask *"everyone"* if they would like to be added.
- Do not be surprised or concerned when some cancel in the future.

Keep an answered-prayer journal.

Encouragement

The tasks involved in your preparation to leave for a new country will overwhelm you if you attempt them all at once, or even think of them together. Each is important, but work on them in their own time.

What if you pick the wrong team? Often the wrong team is the path to the right team, or you learn skills or behaviors to embrace or avoid that God will use with your next team.

What if you do not raise enough support in your allocated time, or at all? View support raising as your final step in discernment—the last door for God to open or close to begin your journey. Do not compare with others raising support—God's plans for each of us are different.

Take each day as it comes. "Therefore do not be anxious about tomorrow, for tomorrow will be anxious for itself. Sufficient for the day is its own trouble." (Matthew 6:34)

The heart of man plans his way, but the LORD establishes his steps.
—Proverbs 16:9

Expect great things from God, attempt great things for God.
—William Carey

Sample Prayer

Lord, please give me wisdom and patience to find a team that will help me to serve you in my new context, who will challenge me to serve you boldly. Please give me the humility to submit to the authority of those whom you have placed over me.

I want to rely on you to provide the financial support I need to fulfill my call. Please be with me on each support call, that my meetings glorify you as you provide for my needs through your servants.

The legal and financial preparations are uncomfortable for me. Please guide me to wise advisors whom I can trust.

Disclaimer

My views and opinions are my own and may or may not align with any entity with which I am now or have been affiliated. They may also not align with your sending agency, fellowship, or company.

Additional Resources

Lanier, Sarah, *Foreign to Familiar* (highly recommended)

McNabb, Dr. Bob, *Spiritual Multiplication in the Real World*

Ramsey, Dave, "Financial Peace University," www.ramseysolutions.com/ramseyplus/financial-peace

Reid, Alvin L. and Malcolm McDow, et al., *Firefall 2.0*

Ripken, Nik, *The Insanity of God*

Shadrach, Steve and Scott Morton, *The God Ask*

Taylor, Dr. and Mrs. Howard, *Hudson Taylor's Spiritual Secret*

Zerub, Caleb, *Nations Prep Handbook*

Notes

Notes

CHAPTER FOUR

LEAVING

Your Final Six Months

… do not be anxious about anything, but in everything by prayer and
supplication with thanksgiving let your requests be made known to God.
And the peace of God, which surpasses all understanding, will
guard your hearts and your minds in Christ Jesus.

—Philippians 4:6-8

Remember, if you fail to prepare, you are preparing to fail.

—Reverend H. K. Williams

You may be anxious or overwhelmed by what is ahead of you. You might question your call. These feelings and doubts are normal—you are not alone.

When confronted with an overwhelming task, Desmond Tutu replied, "How does one go about eating an elephant? … You eat it one bite at a time."

Guiding Principles

- Practice good goodbyes and build your RAFT.
- Prioritize people over things, but say goodbye to places as well.
- Ensure you have no regrets. The enemy hates the work you are leaving to do, and will use hidden sin or unresolved conflict to hurt you and your team, often resulting in leaving the field earlier than planned and an awkward, more difficult reentry into your primary culture.
- Grieve your losses.

Suggestions for your Leaving Phase

Do not neglect your sabbath, time with the Lord, daily diversions, and meeting with friends and family.

Schedule your time.
- Carve out your **sabbath, time with the Lord,** and **time for fun and fellowship.**
- **Set start and end times** for your visits.
  - Be clear that you need to hold to those times.
- **Invite friends or family to help you pack or shop.**
  - You will get additional time with that person and have a decision-making helper while you accomplish your task.
- Build **support raising** into your schedule, if needed.

Build a RAFT[3] to practice "**good goodbyes.**"
- R = **Reconciliation**—Do your part to make amends humbly.
- A = **Affirmation**—Make a point to express your appreciation to those who have meant much to you.
- F = **Farewell**—Say goodbye to people, places, and things.

---

[3]   raisingtcks.com/2014/05/26/how-to-leave-well-build-a-raft/

- o   Add the places you need to visit to your calendar.
- T = **Think Destination**—Allow yourself to get excited.
  - o   Look forward to new favorite places and things.
  - o   Help children think through how major events like birthdays or Christmas will work in your new home.

Have candid discussions with family and close friends.

- Give them **permission to share** their concerns with you.
  - o   **They may feel abandoned**, including adult children and parents.
  - o   Make plans for **regular contact.**
- Parents and grandparents:
  - o   Leave wrapped birthday and Christmas gifts for your children and grandchildren.
  - o   Grandparents, buy two sets of books so you can read to your grandchildren on video calls.

Maintain your **answered-prayer journal.**

Prepare for the unexpected.

- **Visas get delayed, flight plans change**, and **receiving teams change arrival windows.**
  - o   None of these is uncommon.
- **Use this gift of extra time** if it comes.
  - o   Do what you have wanted to do but have not had the time.

Rest! Take a vacation!

Preparing for Departure

It may seem like your departure is far in the future, with plenty of time. These last months will pass quickly—too quickly. The sooner you start, the less stress you will feel if you have time to adjust.

For each window of time below, **review the tasks** in each section and **add them to your calendar** so that you can spread out the work. Methodically prepare so that you depart healthy and rested.

Procrastination is not your friend and will create avoidable angst.

— *Three to Six Months Before Departure* —

Confirm that your **passport is valid for a year** after your planned arrival and that it has at least **twenty blank visa pages**.

- If not, apply for a new one now.
    - Many countries will not accept a passport valid for less than six months after arrival.
    - If you have an option, get one with extra pages.
- **Take four passport photos** with you.
    - You may need them for a visa or other documents.

Confirm visa specifics with your receiving team.

- Start your visa process as soon as possible.
- Requirements change and delays are not uncommon.

Take a vacation!

If you are raising support, stay on track.

Plan your **selling and giving away** room by room.

- **Do one room early** to see how long it takes, and then plan for the rest of the apartment or house.
- **Greed is your enemy.**
    - If you try to maximize the amount for each item you sell, negotiations and delays will add to your stress.
- **Be generous.**
    - Give away as much as you can.

  ○ Let your departure bless others.
- **Build in time** for no-shows, late pickups, and visiting (within reason).

Finalize your "advocacy team" (or "A-Team" as defined in the "Preparing" chapter).
- Start meeting with them.
- Develop rapport and trust before you depart.

Open an **international-friendly bank** account.
- You will probably be in many countries over the next few years.
- A bank that refunds ATM fees is especially helpful.
- You need to ensure you can do international wire transfers into and out of other currencies.

Apply for a **credit card with travel benefits.**
- Look for airport lounge access and Global Entry with Fast Pass (in the U.S.).
- You may benefit from cash-back or travel benefits.
- Good options for those based in the U.S. in 2025 include Chase Reserve and Capital One Venture X.
  - ○ These cards may seem very expensive, but look at the details.
  - ○ Many include refunds on travel to offset the card fees.
  - ○ Look for airport lounge access, which provides respite from the crowds when you are exhausted.

— One to Three Months Before Departure —

Your excitement—and your anxiety—may be increasing. What remains on your to-do list might intimidate you. Schedule tasks to help manage your days.

Pray for peace, mental clarity, and discipline.

Understand your visa.
- If the visa process is relatively quick (for example, a tourist visa for three months acquired online), confirm the details as countries change their rules without notice.
- Confirm **how you acquire it** (online, at the airport, at the embassy before you depart) and **how it is validated** (is there a separate line at the airport or does the embassy in your passport country need to issue it?)

Schedule visits.
- **Block off time** for your family, closest friends, and A-Team first.
- Use an online **scheduling tool** (or shared document or spreadsheet).
  - It may feel insensitive, but most people will understand that you have much to do.
- Kindly **set expectations** that you need to **honor the start and end times.**
- **Do not offer signups during your last week.**

Notify your employer.
- **Provide more notice** than your company requires.
  - Do not put your employer or coworkers in a bind.
  - You may be the only international worker they will ever know, so make a good impression!
- Leave coworkers, customers, and suppliers on good terms.

Assess your wardrobe.
- Take what you **need and love**, and **leave the rest.**
  - If your host country has limited shopping, you will want to take more.
- **Attire may differ** by region of the country or area of the city.
  - Confirm with your receiving team and leaders.
- Do not forget **durable rain gear**, including shoes, even if you move to the desert.
- **Ask your peers** what is and is not available in your host country.
  - Also, ask about the quality relative to what you expect.

- **Support the local economy** when you land.
  - Plan a shopping trip with a colleague after you arrive if necessary.
  - Quality and cost may vary widely.

Carefully review your team's MOU again.
- **Discuss disconnects** with your team leader and adjust your expectations or amend the document.
- **Understand non-negotiable elements.**
  - If they are contrary to your expectations, you will be frustrated.
- **Verbal commitments mean nothing.**
  - If it is not written in the MOU, assume it will not work as you expect it will.
- If your team **does not have an MOU, propose one.**
  - (See the template in the "Contracting" chapter in Part Two.)

Schedule doctor appointments.
- Make appointments early enough to accommodate a follow-on if necessary.
- None the last week before departing, if possible.
- **Discuss preventative medicines or vitamins**—e.g., vitamin D might be a recommendation if you are going somewhere that requires more of your skin to be covered or with little sunshine.

Fill prescriptions.
- Get **at least six months** of necessary medications.
  - Some doctors/pharmacies will provide you with a year.
- Ask if your medication has a different name in your host country, or if there is an alternative available there.
- Ask your team if medicines are **available in your host country.**
  - If not, are they available in a nearby, accessible country?
  - Will there be regular visitors who could bring you refills?

Ensure "**good goodbyes.**"

- Treat **each visit as your last** until your first home assignment.
- **Do not make promises you cannot keep** with certainty, e.g., "I'll definitely see you on my furlough."

Purchase luggage and packing materials.

- ○ See the "Packing" chapter in Part Two for suggestions.

Get a library card to borrow e-books, videos, and audiobooks.

— One Week to One Month Before Departure —

Your move may be years in the making, and here you are in your final month. One day you will look back and this month will be a blur. Hopefully, you followed the advice preceding this chapter and you are not overwhelmed as you complete your final tasks.

A **mix of sadness and excitement is normal**, as is second-guessing your call.

Prepare for the unexpected.

- Do not be surprised if you have days where nothing seems to go right, or if your plans require change at the last minute.
  - ○ Some of your disruptions will be unplanned blessings.
- **Why worry when you can pray?** (Philippians 4:5-7, my paraphrase)
- The evil one does not want you to leave—he does not want the name of Jesus spread.
  - ○ This is true, but is not the source of every disruption.

Complete **travel-related tasks.**

- When you receive approval, **book your flights.**
  - ○ **Avoid multiple airline changes**, if possible.
  - ○ **Avoid short layovers**—you need a minimum of three hours to provide time for delays and transfers.

- ○ **Cheapest is rarely your best choice** with the added stress of your initial move.
    - ■ Pay for a better seat (a middle seat surrounded by strangers could lead to an uncomfortable start to your assignment).
- **Review your visa**, as requirements change.
- Get a **frequent flier account** for each airline you travel.
    - ○ Miles will add up over time and can sometimes be consolidated.
- Get an **international driver's license.**
    - ○ Many countries require them.

Complete **technology-related tasks.**
- **Your phone**
    - ○ Can you roam with your existing plan until you get a local number?
    - ○ Does your host country use eSIMs? Will your phone accept one?
        - ■ Download your eSIM, but recognize most will not work until you land.
    - ○ Is your **phone unlocked?**
        - ■ This surprises people.
        - ■ Locked phones will prevent getting a local number.
    - ○ Plan to port your number to a VOIP-based solution (like Google Voice), and ensure you can send and receive texts for two-factor authentication.
        - ■ Do not port it yet, but this is the time to learn what is needed.
- **Download the apps** you need and **ensure they work**, especially for communications.
    - ○ Check with your receiving team for those they use or require.
- **Establish secure, remote cloud backup.**
    - ○ Start using it now as the initial backup may take a few days.
- Download a **grocery shopping app.**
    - ○ If you are married or have a roommate, use the same one with shared lists.

- ○ Create a list of things you need before you leave.
- ○ Create a list of things you do not want to forget to pack.
- ○ After you arrive in your host country, maintain a list of things you want to get from your home country or want someone to bring you.
- ○ These apps work well for groceries, too!

Plan for departure.

- • **Plan your packing** and purchase anything you still need, such as vacuum bags, favorite toiletries, prescriptions, and luggage.
- • Determine **who will receive your physical mail**.
  - ○ Ideally someone who is unlikely to move while you are away.
  - ○ **Change your accounts** (bank, credit card, etc.) to this address.
  - ○ There are also mail services which charge a monthly fee.
  - ○ Remember to **provide a forwarding address to your postal service.**
- • **Rent an AirBnB or confirm plans** to move in with family or friends the last week or two before you leave.
  - ○ Make sure it is a place **where you can rest.**
  - ○ If friends and family exhaust you, apologize, if necessary, but get the AirBnB.
- • **Schedule final visits**, remembering to reserve your final week for your closest friends and family.

— One Week Before Departure —

Do not overdo this week! Leaving your passport country exhausted and prone to sickness is not an ideal way to start your life in a new country!

Protect your time.

- • **Prioritize your time with the Lord** above all this week.
- • **Preserve this week** for family and your closest friends.
- • **Rest!**

Finalize **travel-related tasks.**

- Make sure you **have your visa.**
- **Contact credit card and debit card providers** to let them know about your travel plans.
- Confirm you have **everything you need to pack** by the beginning of this week.
- **Purchase your eSIM** (if available for your country).
  - Ensure it and any related apps are properly installed.
- **Get cash.**
  - Call your bank ahead of time if you need a lot—they often do not have as much as you might expect.
  - Get some local currency before you leave, if possible.
  - **Keep some global reserve currency** on hand, e.g., 100 USD or 100 EURO.

Pack.

- Pack at the **beginning of this week.**
- Lock all but one checked bag. Live out of this bag and your carry-on bag(s) until you leave (see the "Packing" chapter in Part Two).
- **Weigh luggage** with straps and locks on it.
- Ensure bags are within airline weight restrictions and carry-on bags comply with measurements—some airlines are quite particular.
- **Take your luggage scale.**
  - You will need it for future trips.

— *Two Days Before Departure* —

As your departure approaches, rely on Philippians 4:6-7 and trust in its promise: ". . . do not be anxious about anything, but in everything by prayer and supplication with thanksgiving let your requests be made known to God. And the peace of God, which surpasses all understanding, will guard your hearts and your minds in Christ Jesus."

Protect your time.

- **Prioritize your time with the Lord.** Ask for the peace only he can offer you. Get enough sleep.
- **Decline unplanned requests** for your time, as callous as that sounds.

Finalize travel details.

- Confirm your **flight information.**
- **Confirm departure details**—who will take you to the airport and when?
  - Do not make them wait—be ready early.
  - **Account for traffic.**
  - Plan to **arrive at the airport three hours prior to departure.**
  - Schedule pickup early if your driver tends to run late.
- **Gather necessary arrival information.**
  - Any **tips or tricks for navigating the airport?**
  - How do you **get or validate your visa?**
  - Note a team member's **local address** and **phone number.**
    - This is often needed at passport control.
  - Confirm **who will pick you up.**
    - **Where will you meet?** Does that change if they are delayed or if you are?
    - Ensure they understand **how much luggage** you have.
    - Know **how to reach them using airport Wi-Fi.**
  - If friends/associates are not available, **pay the fee for a reliable driver.**
    - Looking for transportation after arriving jet lagged, especially with children, is stress you do not need on your first day.

Final preparations.

- **Wash clothes.**
  - Make sure they are thoroughly dry before you pack.
  - **Settling in is easier** with a week or two of clean clothes as you learn how life works.
- Gather **travel cash and documents.**

- ○ **Carry a paper copy** of your passport information page, visa, driver's license, and international driver's license.
- ○ **Keep photos of important travel documents on your phone** (especially passport and visa) and **share with anyone traveling with you,** plus a family member or friend not traveling with you.
- ○ **Use a "fanny pack"** for those items you need ready access to, especially your phone, visa, wallet, and passport.
  - ▪ Especially outside of the airport, always carry this in front of you and wear it under a jacket or shirt.
- **Download** music, books, movies, podcasts for the plane and in case of delays.
- **Do not cancel your cell phone** yet if you want to keep your number.

— *Day of Departure* —

You may be nervous, scared, second-guessing your plans, excited, ready to get started, or all of these! **Pray for peace.**

Be ready.
- Have everything by your door **before your pick-up time.**
- Arrive at the airport **at least three hours before departure.**
  - ○ This is not the time to miss flights and inconvenience those helping you.
- **Keep your passport, visa, and other paperwork readily available.**
  - ○ You will need these for check in.
  - ○ Be considerate to those in line behind you.
- Make sure your water bottle is empty before going through security.
- Confirm that your eSIM is set up properly or contact your mobile phone provider to ensure they have roaming options for your host country.

On the plane
- **Drink plenty of water.**
  - ○ Air travel is dehydrating.

- ○ If you do not need to urinate every hour or two, drink more water.
- **Find exercises** you can do in your seat (and do them).
  - ○ At some point during your flight, set your brain to local time (and change your watch).

— *When you Land* —

You are there at last, but not quite there yet. **Pray for the Lord to go before you,** for favor with passport control, baggage claim, and customs. Trust his perfect plans. Smooth or bumpy, easy or stressful, he is in control.

- Review how to **navigate the airport and get your visa.**
- **Keep your paperwork in easy reach.**
- Have something to read in case the passport control or customs lines are slow.
- You will often need an address and phone number for someone local, so have that ready.
- Your first time through **customs and passport control may be unnerving.**
  - ○ **They are just doing their jobs**, and things you packed may be unfamiliar to them.
  - ○ **Do not volunteer information**—only answer questions asked, and do so directly and succinctly.
  - ○ Ensure you **have your STS (Short, Truthful Statement) ready** when asked why you are there.

Contact the person who will pick you up.
- Let them know when you land, when you clear passport control, and after you collect your luggage.
- Let them know if you need to get a SIM card.
- Do you need to exchange cash to tip your porter, or will the person picking you up cover that?
- Do you need money to pay for parking or transportation?

Encouragement

Goodbyes are hard—to your family, your friends, your things, your home, places you love. This can be a sad, confusing, frustrating time, mixed with eager anticipation for the work the Lord has called you to do in a new and exciting place. Grieve each loss, and rely on the Holy Spirit to restore you.

Some will not understand your decisions and may even condemn you. Love them anyway. When Jesus said, "Forgive them for they know not what they do," (Luke 23:34), he modeled this mindset for times like this. People genuinely do not understand.

Spend time with those who will encourage you as you embark on a journey to discover the plans God has for you. Make time for rest, both physical and spiritual. Embrace God's timing.

The LORD bless you and keep you; the LORD make his face to shine upon you and be gracious to you; the LORD lift up his countenance upon you and give you peace.
—Numbers 6:24–26

You do not need a great faith, but faith in a great God.
—James Hudson Taylor

Sample Prayer

Lord, I am tired and anxious. There is so much to do and I feel overwhelmed. I ask you please to send your Comforter to still my racing thoughts, to provide me calm in the chaos, to let my life reflect you. Please give me grace with those I meet, especially those who disagree with my move. Thank you for the opportunity to serve you far away from my home. I ask you for safe travel and to prepare people to hear about you.

Please help me turn to you in prayer and supplication with thanksgiving and find the peace you promise in Philippians 4:5–7. Please go before me in my goodbyes, in my transition, in my packing, in my arrival. Give those who interact with me a glimpse of you.

Disclaimer

My views and opinions are my own and may or may not align with any entity with which I am now or have been affiliated. They may also not align with your sending agency, fellowship, or company.

Additional Resources

Grudem, Wayne, *Systematic Theology*

Lanier, Sandy, *Foreign to Familiar*

Taylor, Dr. and Mrs. Howard, *Hudson Taylor's Spiritual Secret*

Young, Amy, *Getting Started*

Notes

Notes

CHAPTER FIVE

REPORTING

Take my yoke upon you, and learn from me, for I am gentle and lowly in heart, and
you will find rest for your souls. For my yoke is easy, and my burden is light.

—Matthew 11:29–30

There is no lighter burden, nor more agreeable, than a pen.

—Petrarch

Sometime between your preparing phase and arriving, your organization will require some training and you will probably need to claim expenses. With a little advanced planning, you can simplify each of these and reduce your administrative burden. These are for your protection and benefit—embrace them, even if you do not enjoy them.

——————— Guiding Principles ———————

- You are under authority. Do what is asked of you in a timely manner—build in a buffer for unexpected distractions prior to the due date.
- Do not increase the workload on others by making people follow up with you.
- Respect and thank those who help you. Learn how you can simplify their work in how you submit required information.

Required Forms and Training

Every well-run organization has some required training and/or forms. These exist because your organization needs to comply with state, province, or national employment laws and because of their fiduciary responsibility to you and your contributors.

Before you complain, recognize what is required and follow Nike's advertising—"Just Do It."

Add deadlines to your calendar.
- If the requirement says it will take an hour, block off a couple to avoid frustration if it takes longer.
- Get it off of your to-do list as soon as possible so you can focus elsewhere.
- No whining.

Respect those who support you.
- Complete tasks before they are due.
- **Do not be a burden to others** when they have to follow up with you.

Do you think **required tasks are unreasonable?**
- **Ask peers** in other organizations of comparable size and breadth about their requirements.
- If it still seems onerous, discuss with your team leader or organization's human resources (HR) representative.

Expense Reports

These are rarely something people eagerly anticipate, but are necessary for your work.
- Financial stability is part of flourishing.
- **Read your company's policy manual(s).**
  - If you received training as part of your onboarding, review it.
  - Know in advance what can and cannot be expensed, and what receipts are required.

Plan ahead for painless expense claiming.

- **Petrarch's pen** is your phone, laptop, or tablet.
- **Take a picture** of your receipt—immediately.
    - This takes less than thirty seconds.
    - Do it right away, before you lose it.
        - Learn from my mistakes!
- **File it.**
    - Save it to a **dedicated expenses folder.**
    - Use the **filename format** <yy.mm.dd> <Expense Category> <Location> <Amount> < Currency>
        - E.g., I might save this lunch receipt: 24.08.28 Lunch with Jim Bob Supporter -Chez David-23 Euro.
    - **Submit the file format your organization prefers.**
        - Help those who help you.
        - If you do not know, ask—jpg, pdf, etc.
- I email receipts to myself because I keep my expenses in a folder on my laptop.
    - I find it easier to manage documents and file expenses from my computer.

Claim your expenses on time.

- Sort your receipts descending by name.
    - Your most current expenses will be on top.
    - I convert all of mine to .pdf when I create them, which is the format my organization prefers. If I do not convert it, they have to.
- The information you need is in the filename if you follow the advice above.
- You can attach necessary receipts easily.

Build a financial buffer.

- Review and processing will create a lag from the time you claim your expense until it is paid.

- For large expenses in particular, ensure you have enough in your account to cover basic needs like groceries and utilities, or use a credit card so that your reimbursement will arrive before your payment is due.
- If you have unusually large financial needs, talk to your accounting or finance department as far in advance as possible.

Thank your support team (accounting, benefits, training, etc.) every time they help you.

Encouragement

Many are frustrated by "distractions from my important work."

Most who are employed by someone else are required to complete tasks that may seem superfluous but are necessary for an organization's legal and financial stability, as well as their need to meet fiduciary obligations to you and your donors. You should be concerned about your organization's governance and long-term viability if they do not have processes and policies!

The sooner you complete what is required, the sooner you can get back to what you love. You might learn something in the process! I have grumbled my way through a training I thought was unnecessary and found interesting or important information.

> Let all who are under a yoke as [employees] regard their own [employers] as worthy
> of all honor, so that the name of God and the teaching may not be reviled.
>
> —1 Timothy 6:1–2
>
> (I replaced "bondservants" with "employees", and "masters" with "employers")

> I am not a product of my circumstances. I am a product of my decisions.
>
> —Stephen Covey

Sample Prayer

Lord, I am annoyed by these distractions to the work you sent me to do. Help me to honor you and my employer by completing the tasks I do not like thoroughly, accurately, and early. Jesus, you modeled this for me in Matthew 22:21 when you directed your disciple to pay taxes to Caesar. Please replace my grumbling with gratitude and grace. Help me to remember to thank those who ask for corrections or clarifications in the forms and requests I complete.

Disclaimer

My views and opinions are my own and may or may not align with any entity with which I am now or have been affiliated. They may also not align with your sending agency, fellowship, or company.

Additional Resources

Your organization or company's policy manual, field guide, or other recommended documents.

Notes

Notes

CHAPTER SIX

ARRIVING

Your First Six Months

*I have learned in whatever situation I am to be content. I know how to be
brought low, and I know how to abound. In any and every circumstance,
I have learned the secret of facing plenty and hunger, abundance and
need. I can do all things through him who strengthens me.*
—Philippians 4:11b–13

*God seldom calls us for an easier life, but always calls us to know
more of him and drink more deeply of His sustaining grace.*
—John Piper, *Don't Waste Your Life*

Welcome to new sights, sounds, smells, rhythms, and expectations. Some of your new
life will be similar to the life you left. Other aspects will be radically different. This
is the best time to re-dedicate your work to Jesus, to find your identity in him alone.

Guiding Principles

- Give yourself grace and learn from your mistakes. Discover the joy in laughing at yourself.
- Pace yourself. Burnout is another leading cause of unplanned departure. Heed Corrie Ten Boom's warning: "If the devil can't make you sin, he'll make you busy."
- Find a trustworthy guide or mentor from your primary or proximate culture to help you navigate your new environment.
- Listen to your body—seek medical attention early, including telemedicine.
- You should live comfortably, neither as a prince/princess nor a pauper.
- Join a local church in a language you understand well. Establish good spiritual rhythms.

Your First Six Months at a Glance

This first six months will test your resolve and stretch your patience. Your learning curve is steepest during this time as you build your confidence and language skills.

Build your resiliency.
- **Beyond Jesus, you most need flexibility, adaptability, and a sense of humor.**
- **Embrace ambiguity**—you do not know what you do not know.
    - **Ask for help**—from everyone, especially locals.
    - **Do not add hard to hard** because you are too proud to seek help!
- **Do not confuse lack of knowledge for incompetence.**
    - You are working your way up your learning curve.
    - Treat every new challenge as a **learning opportunity.**
    - You did not become incompetent overnight—your cognitive processing may be adversely impacted by decision fatigue, jetlag, and language-learning fog.
- **Seek deep relationships**—you need them, even if they may be short-lived!

- Grieve current relationships that deteriorate due to time zones and distance.
- You often find these through common interests or hobbies.
- **Do not compare**
  - Language acumen, local friends, meals in local homes, or anything else.
  - God's plan for you is uniquely yours.
  - What he plans for you may or may not be related to the work you do.

You are responsible for your care!

- For additional details, see the "Self-Care" chapter.
- Build rhythms to contact those in your **circles of care**.
- Your team may be **your only "friends"** initially, even though they may not be the friends you would have picked from a larger pool.
  - Your team may fall short of your expectations, and your role will probably differ from what you think—prepare to adapt.
- Find community outside your team if possible (church, other expatriates, or a hobby)—it will not find you.

Become a problem solver.

- **Search for solutions** before you accept, and complain about, inconveniences.
- **Become a resource** for your team and others.
  - **Share what you learn.**
    - Others are also struggling, or have been.
  - Anecdote: Our internet was slow. I talked to the provider and learned the speed varies by time of day, so I downloaded large files early in the morning, and shared this information with my team.
- Not every inconvenience is from the devil.
  - Sometimes the internet goes down.
  - Wet marble is slippery.
  - What is unusual and uncomfortable for you is the local person's normal.
- **Approach every challenge as an opportunity to grow and trust.**

Set reasonable expectations.

- **You may love your team, and you may not.**
  - They cannot meet all your needs.
- **Plan to accomplish less** than you did where you lived last.
  - Language barriers, transportation, different processes, and, in some contexts, corruption or bureaucracy will slow you down.
  - **Learn what is reasonable** to complete in a day—or a week—ask others!
  - **Be willing to pay** a local for some tasks.
    - Weigh which is more valuable in the moment—your time or your money.
    - Support your local economy and meet new people.
    - **Single females:** Ask friends or team members (especially those with better language skills) to join you when people come to your home to work.
- Locals in some countries **do not honor agreements** (or may not with expatriates).
- **Minor health issues are common** due to new foods, different water, and airborne pollutants.
  - If they are severe or last significantly longer than your peers, seek medical attention.
- When you **talk to friends and family** you left:
  - Expect to **listen more than you speak** to reduce disappointment.
  - Ask good questions.
  - **Seek to understand, not to be understood.**[4]
    - Their lives are also changing.

Begin your language-learning journey.

- Full-time language acquisition is typical for one's first several months to few years.

---

[4] From the "Prayer of St. Francis," though that prayer was not actually written by St. Francis.

- Studying a new language makes many people **tired and hungry.**
- Most people **feel incompetent,** to some degree,
  - Despite a college degree and/or work experience.
  - Some are naturals, and others (like me) will never find fluency.
- **Find the language-learning style that works for you** if you have options.
  - People learn differently.
- **Pray before each session.**
  - This made a significant difference for us.

Establish your digital footprint.
- Conform to your **team's norms** and **security protocols.**
  - This is for your safety and that of the rest of the team.
- Establish **"public" and "private" identities.**
  - **Exclusive use of "secure" communications** may lead local authorities to question your continued presence.
  - You need to use secure communications for some topics.
  - However, you need a presence using the tools common to your host country.
  - Your team will help you navigate the difference.

———— Your First Six Months: Phase by Phase ————

The following sections will help you know what you need to do and what to expect.

— *Your First Few Days* —

- **Confirm your pickup,** either friends, coworkers, or a trusted, reliable car hire.
- Give yourself a few days to recover from jetlag.
- **Ask questions!**
  - Set your pride aside.
  - **Do not struggle unnecessarily** because you are worried that you will seem incapable (you are!).

- **Do not become a victim** and a burden to your team due to ignorance.
  - Are there protocols your team has established for your safety?
  - Are there places you should avoid?

— *Your First Week* —

- **Under-schedule your days.**
- **Ask more questions.**
  - What are the **team rules?** (Review the **MOU.**)
  - How are team decisions made, and by whom?
  - Are there foods you need to avoid?
  - Should you take taxis, Uber, public transportation, or walk?
  - Should you walk or ride alone or only with others you trust?
  - Can you drink the water? Brush your teeth with it? Cook with it?
  - Can you flush the toilet paper?
  - Understand your **team's evacuation plan** and make necessary preparations (if relevant for your content), including packing a **"go bag."**

Celebrate wins.

— *Your First Month* —

By this point, you should be able to **find more answers on your own.**

Make your house your home.
- **Your home needs to be a haven** to return to each day.
- Your time investment now will benefit you during your entire stay, regardless of duration.
- Find a home that is comfortable, especially during full-time language learning.
  - You will have time to "live local" soon enough.
- Put up pictures, even if you plan to move frequently.
- Be reasonable—you should not live like a pauper, nor a prince or princess.

- ○ You get **no extra credit for sub-standard living**, and such a lifestyle may inhibit your ministry.[5]

Create a schedule.
- You will find you waste time if you do not.
- Build in **sabbath rhythms**.
- Separate **work and personal time**.
  - ○ Your weekends need to be time for refreshment and worship.
  - ○ If you have work requirements in the evenings, adjust your days.
  - ○ Failure to do this puts you on the burnout path.
- Initially, most of your workday will revolve around language study.
- Remember to build in time for transportation, shopping, and cooking.
  - ○ Many underestimate how long these things take in a new culture!

Focus on transactional language.
- What you will need most are greetings, how to make purchases, and give directions.
  - ○ **Laugh at your mistakes.**
    - ▪ Anecdote: We asked for five frogs instead of apples, and still get a laugh remembering the grocer's confused expression.
  - ○ One day soon, what you have learned will amaze you.

Build your network.
- Develop your **accountability network**.
  - ○ Find someone in your same context but **not on your team**.
  - ○ You need someone with whom you can be completely open, especially regarding team or leadership challenges.
- Build your list of **medical providers**.
  - ○ If your team does not have a list already, start one and share it.
  - ○ Embassies may maintain lists.

---

[5] supportraisingsolutions.org/five-reasons-poor-talk-killing-ministry/

    ○   Ask other teams or friends at NGOs.

Worship.

- **Join a theologically sound church,** if one is available and safe to attend.
  - Do not join a church for "strategic" reasons, like a place to take locals or network.
    - **Church is for teaching and worship.**
    - Worship in a language you understand well.
    - Those other things are side benefits, but cannot be your intent.
  - Do not attend services to "learn spiritual language."
    - This is not the purpose of church.
    - You might attend a second service for this purpose.
- **You need community beyond your team** in a natural language right now.

Communicate.

- **Send your newsletter** regularly.
  - Develop the habit now.
  - (See the "Writing Newsletters" chapter in Part Two for more details.)
- **Transfer your prior-country phone number** to an internet phone service (like Google Voice) if you want to retain it.

Celebrate wins.

— *Your First Three Months* —

Become increasingly independent.

- Find more answers on your own.
- **Some struggle** is an effective teacher.
  - **Exasperation** when others can help you is either pride or foolishness.

Set aside a full day each month.

- **Rest, reflect, and connect** with God.

- **Plan your next month.**
  - ○ Adjust your daily and weekly rhythms as needed.
- This is a workday, not a vacation day.
- Do not study language this day.
- Continue this discipline throughout your term on the field.

Continue **language study.**

Extend your network.
- Meet people in different organizations and on different teams.
- **You need friends with whom you do not need to translate.**
  - ○ You need their perspective and outside input for what is "normal."
  - ○ Most may be from a culture similar to yours in this phase.
- **Develop friendships with locals.**
  - ○ These people will probably speak your native or second language, like a language teacher.

Pursue your hobby or develop a new one.

Leave the country for a weekend if you live in a challenging environment.
- Follow team policies.
- You might need a visa run, anyway.
- Where good medical care is not available, many make "medical visa runs" when needed.

Celebrate wins.

— *Your First Six Months* —

Further extend your network.
- You should have some **local acquaintances** by now, if not friends.
  - ○ If not, redouble your efforts and pray for God to lead you to them.

- Schedule "enculturation" days where you set goals outside of your comfort zone to learn how to do something local (ride a bus if it is safe), participate in a local festival (if not related to idol worship), find a cooking class or learn a local craft.

The wall.
- Not one of Pink Floyd's bricks.
- Many people **"hit a wall"** about now.
  - Those **things you loved** when you first arrived, **you love no longer.**
  - The things that excited you leave you flat.
  - Anywhere seems better than where you are.
  - **This is normal,** even if your host culture is similar to the one you left!
  - **This will pass,** but may take a few days or weeks.

Schedule a multi-day debrief around your six-month anniversary.

Language acquisition may continue to consume most of your work days.
- Even so, scale back a bit to carve time to **do what you came to do.**
  - Your **language acquisition will benefit** as you learn local words applicable to your work.
  - Your weeks will be less frustrating.
- Some hire a tutor to focus on specific language needs (spiritual, medical, business, engineering, etc.).

Schedule days to learn about your local culture.
- Challenge yourself to leave your comfort zone.
- Partner with another team member or member of another team, especially someone who has been there longer.
- Where it is safe, learn how to take a bus, visit local markets, create a scavenger hunt for your team to find local treasures or try local experiences, etc.

Celebrate wins.

- Schedule an event with your team to share together.
- Celebrate with those who receive your newsletter.

Encouragement

Starting life in a third culture can present challenges you never imagined. Do not make it harder than it needs to be. Ask for help—from your teammates, other language students, people in your church, or new acquaintances.

When you move to a third culture for work, study, or ministry, you will not be the first to cry because you feel like an idiot studying a new language. Cultural differences may never make sense to you, and will lead you to laugh, cry, shake your fist, scream, or want to leave—maybe all in the same day.

When you hit a wall and cannot see forward, reflect on how far you have come. Celebrate little wins—and big ones. You will be successful again. I pray you will find sufficiency in Jesus during the times he is all you have. He who called you is faithful.

I will never leave you nor forsake you.

—Hebrews 13:5b

Send me anywhere, only go with me. Lay any burden on me, only sustain me.
Sever any tie, but the ties that bind me to your service and to your heart.

—David Livingstone

Sample Prayer

Lord, sometimes I question why I came—why you sent me. The things I loved, now I despise. I will not be able to continue without your help. Please sustain me through this dry period and return my sense of purpose and love for this place and these people.

I need your help as I study language. Some days I feel like an incapable child.

Please help me not to confuse wants and needs, unnecessary but familiar comforts with the provision that will sustain me as this becomes my new home.

Disclaimer

My views and opinions are my own and may or may not align with any entity with which I am now or have been affiliated. They may also not align with your sending agency, fellowship, or company.

Additional Resources

Corbett, Steve and Brian Fikkert, *When Helping Hurts*

Corbett, Steve, Brian Fikkert, and Katie Casselberry, *Helping Without Hurting in Church Benevolence*

Grudem, Wayne, *Systematic Theology*

Lanier, Sandy, *Foreign to Familiar*

Young, Amy, *Getting Started*

—————————————— Notes ——————————————

Notes

CHAPTER SEVEN

STAYING

Trust in the LORD, and do good; dwell in the land and befriend faithfulness.
Delight yourself in the LORD, and he will give you the desires of your
heart. Commit your way to the LORD; trust in him, and he will act.

—Psalm 37:3–5

It is always possible to be thankful for what is given rather than to complain
about what is not given. One or the other becomes a habit of life.

—Elisabeth Elliot

As time passes, your host country may become more familiar than your passport country. Your host country may be the only "home" your children know. In this period, I pray the words from this hymn reflect where you find your strength:

My hope is built on nothing less
Than Jesus' blood and righteousness
I dare not trust the sweetest frame
But wholly lean on Jesus' name

On Christ the solid rock I stand
All other ground is sinking sand.[6]

If you are in full-time ministry and Jesus is not the source of your identity and grounding, you will reach a point of failure living in a country where you will never be fully accepted. You will find that you love and despise your host country at the same time. This paradox is normal.

Singleness, marriage, and parenting contribute differently to long-term flourishing. Read about these in Part Two "Topical Information and Advice" section.

Guiding Principles

- Your priorities must be God, family, then work.
- Ensure your time reflects your commitments and priorities.
- Develop close relationships, though people will come and go.
- Rest—take vacation and sabbath.
- Practice self-care.

Build Relationships

Develop relationships, though they may be short-lived.

- **People come and go often** in cross-cultural ministry and other work with expatriates due to embassy and NGO terms and ministry needs.
- It is better to enjoy several good but short relationships than none.
  - You do not know when your paths may cross again.
- **Close, meaningful relationships with locals** connect you to your location and increase your desire to stay when you find your new culture difficult.

---

6   Mote, Edward. "My Hope is Built on Nothing Less." Hymns of Praise, A New Selection of Gospel Hymns, Combining All the Excellencies of our Spiritual Poets, with Many Originals, 1837.

Do not compare spiritual fruit.

- Some quote **five, seven, or nine years** to produce spiritual fruit.
    - Do not let averages distract you.
    - Anecdote: I know workers who experienced **abundant fruit in two weeks**, and others saw **one person come to faith in twelve years.**
- **Do the work** God has called you to do.
    - His plan for you is unique to you.
    - **Leave the fruit to him.**
- Read about Jim Elliot[7] and others in cross-cultural ministry throughout time to encourage your trust in the Lord's timing for the fruit of your labors.

Find an **accountability partner.**

- Look for someone in your **same context but not on your team**, someone with whom you can share completely.
- **Sin tendency is magnified** on the field.
    - The enemy hates the work you do.
    - Find someone who will help you address temptations and failures.
- Your team may also provide accountability, but most find they cannot share everything because some challenges result from team dynamics.

———— Align Your Work with Your Priorities ————

Do not overestimate your importance.

- "We are not building God's kingdom. He is building his kingdom, and we are praying for the privilege of being involved." - Francis Schaeffer
- For couples and parents: **Your spouse and children need you!**
    - God can raise up workers from rocks, but your family only has one of you.

Keep learning!

---

[7] elisabethelliot.org/about/Jim-Elliot/

Engage in your work.
- Do not let your nascent language skills deter you from the work you were sent to do.
- **Partner with another expatriate or local partner** to model for you.
  - Your time with a mentor will show how the **theory you learned** (or think you learned) works in practice.
- The shift from "full-time language" tends to be fulfilling and energizing—and will **help you endure and prepare** for the future.

Align your tasks with your stated priorities.
- Priority is often stated as: abiding, then sharing, then language, then administrative tasks.
- Tasks are often prioritized from administrative, then language, then sharing, then abiding.
- **Track your time** in thirty-minute intervals for two weeks to determine if your practice aligns with your plans.
- Early in your first term, or after moving to a new country, language often consumes an out-sized focus to prepare in the initial months or few years, so measure the non-language time.

Prevent scope creep for you and others.
- If your days are full, do not take on new tasks without releasing others.
- Corrie ten Boom said, "If Satan can't make you bad, he'll make you busy" (my paraphrase).
- Scope creep leads to **burnout.**

Change teams if necessary.
- Many find that how they want to serve changes as knowledge, skills, and relationships develop.
- **Your vision** must align with your team's.
  - If it does not, you may need to change teams.
  - Discuss with your team leader and sending fellowship.

- The team you want to join may be aligned with a different organization.
  - This is normal and fairly common—and does not necessarily imply any problem with your prior team.
- If you change teams, determine if you can **second** (pronounced "se kond") to them.
  - **Secondment:** your "employer of record" is one organization, but functionally you lead are on a team that is part of a different organization.
    - You attend "their" conferences, and follow "their" policies.
  - If you are supported by a number of different individuals or entities, this avoids the need to transfer them to a new organization.
  - You still need to communicate your new work and/or new team to your supporters.

Work yourself out of your job.
- Replace yourself with a local partner, if possible.
- This helps **prevent your mission from becoming your idol.**

Simplify the boring stuff.
- Finances, reimbursements, operational stuff—make it easy.
- Read the "Reporting" chapter in Part One.
- Use a **shared calendar** with your roommate(s) or spouse.
  - It is helpful in scheduling and for security to know where someone should be.
- Continue your contributions to a retirement plan.
  - Talk to a financial planner for details.

——————— Stay the Course ———————

You were called by a good God to serve in a new place, which may be uncomfortable, challenging, and/or difficult.

- **Attitude matters**—you cannot determine what will happen during your days, but you have total control over how you respond.
- 1 Thessalonians 5:16-18 says, "Rejoice always, pray without ceasing, give thanks in all circumstances; for this is the will of God in Christ Jesus for you."
  - Rejoicing when you do not want to, and giving thanks for those situations you would rather avoid, will change your heart and your attitude.
  - You are not alone—pray that the Holy Spirit will help you live these verses.
- **Replace "but" with "and."**
  - Replace "I love the people, but I hate the traffic," with "I love the people and hate the traffic."
  - Replace "I love the food, but despise going to the market," with "I love the food and despise going to the market."
  - These paradoxes are normal—using "and" helps you embrace the conflicting feelings.

Initial terms typically vary from **two to five years.**
- Many organizations **discourage routine passport/home country visits** during the first year to the full first term.
  - Frequent visits make the challenges of adaptation more difficult.
  - Funerals, weddings, and severe illness for immediate family members are common exceptions.
- Pray for endurance and God's love for your team and the people you were sent to serve.
  - It takes a few years for your new culture to be familiar and feel like home, but for most people, it does.
  - Expect disappointment and missed expectations—allow God to use these to draw you closer to himself.
- Talk to others, both in your context and those on your advocacy team.
  - Reconsider discussing your discomfort with those who did not want you to go, as they will add to your dissatisfaction.

- If you are in the "ongoing" phase of your work.
  - ○ **Set a commitment period.**
  - ○ As you approach that date, honestly and humbly stop and reflect on your effectiveness.
  - ○ Listen to God to determine if you:
    - Stay in the same place doing the same work
    - Stay in the same place doing different work
    - Change locations but do the same work
    - Change your location and work (including exiting ministry or retiring)

──────────── **Rest and Reflect** ────────────

Use your vacation days—all of them!
- You are not so important that your team or organization cannot be without you for a couple of weeks.
- You need the time to unplug completely—avoid "staycations" if possible.

Enjoy your hobby (or develop a new one).
- **Make time for fun.**
- **You need balance**—do something you love every day, even for a few minutes.
- **Be sensitive to local norms.**
  - ○ Sunbathing for a woman in a conservative Muslim culture might not be the best hobby choice.

For those who **live in a difficult context:**
- Leave your host country regularly (every three to six months).
- You are not a hero **for pushing through.**
  - ○ Your host country may never be your normal, and you may need some of your "old normal" occasionally.

Attend important events in your passport country.

- You will miss many events (birthdays, graduations), but attend the biggest ones, which include, but are not limited to:
  - Marriage of immediate family member, maybe best friend
  - First child born to or adopted by a sibling
  - Death of immediate family member
- **Weigh the impact** of missing key events on others.
  - The sacrifice may add tremendous credibility to your ministry, that you are willing to sacrifice for those you serve.
  - Absence might have a negative impact on those to whom you minister abroad and/or your extended family who highly value family relationships.
  - Will the reconnection with family and friends may be encouraging or painful?
  - Evaluate the costs and benefits with close friends, mentors, and spiritual leaders.

Complete a **multi-day debrief** every few years.
- These are generally three to five days.
- It sounds like a long commitment, but it takes that long to fully process your experience.
  - Also, complete one when you change teams or countries.
- A debrief helps you close your current assignment and prepares you to launch into your new one.

Sabbatical
- If you and your organization agree on a sabbatical:
- Agree on purpose and timeframe:
  - One to six months to **disconnect and rest** are common.
  - Clarify your purpose: fresh vision and new ideas help free you to determine what you start, stop, or continue when you return, or to prepare you mentally and emotionally for a new assignment.
- Find a coach to help you prepare and execute this specific type of leave.

Self-Care

You are responsible for your care!
- Do not become complacent and overlook self-care needs.
- Review the "Self-Care" chapter in Part Two for a complete discussion.

Address leadership challenges early.
- You will not find (or be) a perfect leader.
- Overlook personality differences and minor offenses (Proverbs 19:11).
- When there is conflict, start with the process described in Matthew 18:15–20.
- Your relationships with those on other teams will provide a framework for what is healthy and what is not, but avoid gossip.
- If you suspect **spiritual abuse:**
  - Visit https://michaeljkruger.com/what-is-spiritual-abuse/ or read chapter 2 of *Bully Pulpit* to learn more.
  - Discuss your concerns with a trusted spiritual leader.

Encouragement

This may become one of the richest periods of your life, the phase where God uses the gifts he has given you to serve others and reap rewards you never imagined, to bless you and others through you in astounding ways. It may also be a period of prolonged stress that results in physical ailments.

Your dependence on God will grow tremendously while you are on the field, with so much out of your control. Whether you serve a few months, the rest of your life, or any period in between, if you "Delight yourself in the Lord ... he will give you the desires of your heart." (Psalm 37:4) His purpose for you may not be anything you expected when you started, but when you align your heart with his, you will find the joy he promises.

And let us not grow weary of doing good, for in due
season we will reap if we do not give up.

—Galatians 6:9

*If a commission by an earthly king is considered an honor, how can
a commission by a Heavenly King be considered a sacrifice?*

—David Livingstone

Sample Prayer

Lord, for as long as I am here, show me how to live my life to reflect you; let my life be a draw to others, to open a door to share your story. Please give me grace towards those things in this culture that annoy or perplex me and those who perpetrate them, patience to endure tasks that could be more efficient, and vision to see how to bless those in my sphere of influence to your glory alone.

Lead me to people who will become friends and show me how to glorify you when I talk to family and friends in the country I left who do not understand why I am here.

Disclaimer

*My views and opinions are my own and may or may not align with
any entity with which I am now or have been affiliated. They may also
not align with your sending agency, fellowship, or company.*

Additional Resources

Alma, Carissa, *Thriving in Cross-Cultural Ministry*

Corbett, Steve, and Brian Fikkert, *When Helping Hurts*

Corbett, Steve, Brian Fikkert, and Katie Casselberry, *Helping Without Hurting in Church Benevolence*

Eenigenburg, Sue and Eva Burkholder, *Grit to Stay Grace to Go*

Grudem, Wayne, *Systematic Theology*

Kruger, Michael J., *Bully Pulpit*

McKie, Rusty, *Sabbaticals*

Reid, Alvin L., Malcolm McDow, et al., *Firefall 2.0*

Notes

Notes

CHAPTER EIGHT

VISITING

Furlough, Home Leave

Do not neglect to show hospitality to strangers, for thereby
some have entertained angels unawares.

—Hebrews 13:2

O divine Master, grant that I may not so much seek
to be consoled as to console,
to be understood as to understand,
to be loved as to love.

—Anonymous,
attributed (erroneously) to St. Francis of Assisi

Most people working cross-culturally typically return to their passport country for an extended period at regular intervals (typically one to five years). This has various names, including furlough, home leave, home ministry assignment, etc.

The length of one's first assignment often varies from one to four years, and the first home leave at the end of that period varies from a month to a year. The details should be clear and agreed to in your MOU.

This is not the same as a sabbatical, which has a different purpose. See the "Staying" chapter in Part One for more information about sabbaticals.

Fight for your Sabbath rest and time with the Lord. It is easy to get too busy. Do not give the devil a foothold.

Guiding Principles

- Be a great guest.
- Give more than you ask.
- Plan ahead and be prepared.
- Your expectations will be tested. Be clear with yourself and others.

Purpose

Purposes vary, but include some mix of these elements:

- Rest, refreshment, and reunion
- Raising support
- Renewing relationships with sending fellowships or individuals
- Visa renewal
- A home leave is not merely an extended vacation.

Understand what your organization, sending fellowship, and/or sending agency expects from this visit. Include them in your planning.

Expectations

You may plan on a huge reception with a ticker-tape parade, lavish accommodation, exotic meals, and an eager, listening audience. This would be a good time to reset your expectations.

Invest in those closest to you.

- Give them extra grace.
- Take time to help them learn what to ask and how to listen.

Prepare for excitement and disappointment.

- It may not be a parade, but most people will be excited to see you.
  - ○ Those who are most excited may surprise you.
  - ○ Those who will not make time for you may lead to disappointment.

You will not return to the place you left.

- At least, not exactly.
  - ○ Friends may have moved or moved on.
  - ○ Favorite places may be closed or changed.
- Anecdote: After a two-year hiatus, we moved back into our same home, in the same neighborhood, rejoined the same church, expecting to step right back into the life we left, but none of it was the same!
  - ○ **We were unprepared.**
  - ○ **I want to help you be prepared.**
    - ■ Yes, I was a Boy Scout and a Scout leader.
- Many experience "**reverse culture shock**," which may increase as the time between visits increases.
- Talk to friends in your passport country to learn what has changed before your return to help minimize this adjustment.

Most people cannot understand the life you live.

- Nor does everyone need to know everything.
- Some may not understand why you are in your host country.
- **People do not know what to ask you.**
  - ○ **Expect most questions to be superficial.**
  - ○ Questions you may hear:
    - ■ "How was your trip?" though you have been gone for years.
    - ■ "How is <country>?" which is not where you live.

- "Aren't you glad to be home where you are safe?" though it may not be home any longer and you feel safer in your host country.
  - **Help those meeting with you!**
    - Practice an "**elevator pitch**" in which you can summarize your life abroad and future plans in a few well-structured sentences—no more than two to three minutes.
  - **Ask good questions** and **model how to listen!**
    - They might get the hint and ask them of you in return! Some sample questions:
    - "In the past <x> years, what significant changes have happened in your life?"
    - "What do you most enjoy now?"
    - "How are you most challenged or frustrated?"
    - "Where do you see God most active in your life?"

You Are an Ambassador

These are lessons I was either taught by those who went before me, learned through my experience as one who returned for home leave, or learned when we hosted people on their home leaves. I do not know what you know, so please forgive me if you know all of this already. Based on our experience providing hospitality, many do not.

You represent us all.
- You may be the only cross-cultural ministry worker your host has ever met.
- Your conduct may open the door for your host to follow in your footsteps one day, create a desire to support other international workers, or promote missions to others.
- Your conduct may also close that door.
- Model what it looks like to **depend on your savior alone for your sense of worth.**
  - Value others above yourself, including parents and siblings.
- Some missionaries return and **expect the world to revolve around them.**

- ○ Please do not be that person!
- ○ **Invest in your host.**
- ○ **Take a genuine interest** in them, even if it means you share less than you hope.
- **Avoid extravagant requests**, which may lead your host to question how you steward their investment in you, which may make them jaded towards others as well.

— Be an Exceptional House Guest —

Understand expectations.
- **Take a gift** (does not need to be exorbitant) **and a card** from your host country on which to write your thank-you note.
- Ask **what your host expects.**
  - ○ Can you sleep until noon, or do they expect you at breakfast at 7:00 a.m.?
  - ○ Honor your host by adapting to their schedule.
- Respect **time restrictions** or **curfews.**
  - ○ Your host may rise early for work or have children who go to sleep early.
- **Ask permission.**
  - ○ Do not assume everything is available to you.
  - ○ What food and drinks are available to you?
  - ○ When asked, "Is there anything else you need?" be judicious with your answer.
  - ○ Are you allowed to have guests? If so, any limitations?
- **Discuss schedule expectations**, especially with family members.
  - ○ People close to you may expect you to be available all day, every day.
  - ○ You may need to raise support and visit supporters, do training or counseling, or meet with your sending church or organization.
  - ○ Discuss your schedule with those close to you before you arrive.
- **Return a car** loaned to you clean and full of gas.

Do you need an AirBnB, parsonage, or other housing option?

- Do you need **time to rest and disconnect** away from people?
- **Be honest with your family and friends**—kind, but honest.
    - The best way for you to be a good guest may be not to be one, for at least part of your stay.

— Be a Conscientious Dining Guest —

Supporters often want to host you for a meal in their home or at a restaurant.

Dining in someone's home

- If they ask what you want,
    - **Ask for options, or their favorite dishes to make.**
    - They may be thinking of soup and you may want a six-course meal, so asking is a gentle way to understand their frame of reference.
    - Do not answer "anything" unless you actually mean it.
        - You do not want your host to spend time making something you cannot eat or do not like.
        - Your host desires to serve you.

Dining in a restaurant

- Ask what they normally order to **gauge the expense** of the dish you should order.
    - You do not need to dine on crackers and water, nor do you want to order filet mignon with lobster when they order an inexpensive salad.
    - If pressured to order something more expensive, you have more freedom, but still exercise some restraint.
    - Another good consideration: If you were paying for your meal (and not being reimbursed), what would you order?

--- **Prepare** ---

If your time in your passport country is a month or longer, you may think you will have more time than you need, but it will pass surprisingly fast.

Plan.

- Heed Benjamin Franklin's warning: "Those who fail to plan are planning to fail."
- **If you are not a planner, ask for help** from a friend or supporter who is.
- Schedule a **planning retreat.**
    - Allocate a few days, at least three months before your departure.
    - Spend half the time with a calendar scheduling visits and tasks to complete, and the other half relaxing.

Schedule appointments.

- **Medical exams** and tests may require at least six months to schedule.
    - Schedule early in your stay to leave time for a follow-up, if required.
- Make **appointments for children.**
    - If they have behavioral, speech, or sensory issues, a professional evaluation will help you determine the best path forward.
    - Allow time to begin necessary treatment and get a plan that you can do when you return to the field (if the severity is minor enough).
- Older children may need separate time with their friends.

Prepare for speaking engagements.

- Be selective in what opportunities you accept.
    - Offer less-formal engagements like question-and-answer sessions as an alternative if you are not a natural public speaker.
- Determine your allotted time.
    - **Do not go over your time limit.**
    - **Practice** until you are at least ten percent under the allotted time.
- Your audience does not need to hear everything you know.

- **Limit anecdotes.**
  - ○ Leave most of those for individual or small group interactions.
- Speaking longer than you are offered is disrespectful to your host and audience.

Arrange for a debrief.
- This would ideally be residential.
- Try to complete it before you go or soon after arrival.
  - ○ You need someone to hear your story.
  - ○ Most in your home country will not have the capacity to listen.

— How to Allocate Your Time —

Most home visits are not purely vacations. Many organizations or sending fellowships expect you to do something related to your work. If this is you, the following may help.

A good time allocation plan is:
- **30% rest and reunion** (time with family and friends plus other fills like vacation)
- **30% personal growth and health** (doctor's appointments, counseling, debriefing, continuing education)
- **40% ministry** (raising support, connecting with supporters, connecting with overseas partners)

Plan visits with friends, family, and supporters ahead of your visit.
- First, carve out time for those **closest to you.**
- Then **use a scheduling application** or shared online document or spreadsheet so people can sign up on their own.
  - ○ **Do not rely on messaging and emails** to schedule time with people—it will wear you out and you will miss appointments.
  - ○ It may seem a bit corporate, but it will help you honor your commitments and fit everyone in.

- Offer as many opportunities as possible, probably three or four a day in two-hour increments with an hour for travel in between.
    - They will not all be filled, so do not stress.
    - Set your availability to preserve time for rest and necessary appointments.
    - Do not accommodate unreasonable requests—try to find common ground but realize you may miss some people.
- Set expectations that you will **hold to the time** to honor those who come after and to preserve your health.
- Anecdote: We did not schedule over a meal because we did not want people to think we expected them to feed us.
    - Some asked to meet a bit earlier or later so that they could provide a meal, which we accepted whenever we could.

— Preparing for Departure from your Host Country —

If you complete your tasks over time, you will be under less stress.

— Two to Three Months Prior to Departure —

Communicate.
- **Send your tentative schedule to** your pastor or other church leader, advocacy team, and family for feedback.
- Work with your church, sending agency, family, and advocacy team for **lodging, car, and other needs.**
- Set up necessary **doctor appointments** (ideally six months prior to departure).

Complete forms, reservations, and applications.
- If you are U.S.-based and will return at least once a year, apply for Global Entry.
- Complete **any forms required** by your organization or sending fellowship.
- Schedule your **trips/vacations.**

Confirm and gather feedback.
- **Book flights and lodging.**
- **Confirm appointments** and vacation plans.

Communicate your needs if you have raised your own support.
- When you send your regular newsletter, **if you need finances, ask!**
  - Specify if your need is one-off (e.g., for travel) or for ongoing needs.
  - Ask those who support you already if their financial situation has changed so that they could increase their support for you.
  - Ask your supporters for names of others who might be interested in supporting you.
- Update your support presentation for new supporters or those who want to learn more.

Complete tasks.
- Start a list of things you need to purchase to take back to your host country and ensure you have funds in your budget.
  - Many purchase small gifts for language teachers, neighbors, and local friends.
- **Start looking for small gifts and cards** from your host country for support visits and those who loan you a car and host you in their home.

— One Month Prior to Departure —

Communicate.
- Schedule **one-on-one meetings** with those closest to you.
- **Notify your pastor** or other church leader of your plans.

Schedule visits.
- **Confirm one-on-one visits** with those closest to you.
- **Schedule group visits.**

- ○ **Offer a mix of environments**—for example, after church in a classroom, at a park for families, at a restaurant for lunch.
  - ○ Schedule with **small affinity groups** (mutual friends, Sunday school classes, former teams, etc.) to reduce the number of visits and see more people.
- **Create a sign up** for additional one-on-one visits with supporters.

Repeat your support ask, if necessary.

Buy gifts and cards or postcards for family/supporters/hosts.
- Ensure you have cards or post cards for thank-you notes.
- People tend to love small, useful, inexpensive, handmade, local items, such as coasters, bookmarks, and magnets.
  - ○ Most people do not need more dust collectors.
- Your host might appreciate a gift of service—cook, clean, do yard work, watch their children.

Prepare to leave your current location.
- **If you will not return, assume each goodbye will be your last.** (Read the "Returning" chapter.)
  - ○ Say goodbye to special places as well.
- **If you will return** to your same home:
  - ○ **Make financial arrangements for local providers** who depend on you for income.
  - ○ Arrange to **leave your key** with someone who will check on your home.

— Two Weeks Prior to Departure —

Send a sign-up reminder for group and one-on-one/small group events.

Pay any bills that will come due in your absence if you cannot pay them remotely or leave money with someone who will pay them.

Confirm who will take you to and pick you up from the airport, and your first place to stay.

— *Last Week Prior to Departure* —

If you plan to return to the same home in your host country:
- **Turn off water and electricity** (except refrigerator, unless you will leave it empty, then leave the doors open).
- **Cover furniture** to keep off dirt and dust.
- Plan so that team ministries are not drastically affected.
- Arrange for **someone to pay those dependent on you** for income.
- **Close exterior blinds** if you have them.

Encouragement

If you approach your time away with realistic plans, good communication, and an attitude of "What can I give" rather than "What can I get," you avoid disappointment caused by missed expectations. Add in time for rest and fill from God and close friends to create the best opportunity for a great visit.

Most people will not fully understand what you have done and what the life you have lived. Some may be confrontational. Remember who called you and whom you serve.

A multi-day debrief before you depart or early in your stay will help you work through your first term on the field, give you a place to be fully heard, and relieve the frustration of conversations with those whom you love but who do not have the capacity or understanding to listen fully.

Rest, do something fun, and intersperse difficult visits with fulfilling ones. Decide to enjoy each day. You do not get to choose what happens, but you are fully in control of how you respond.

… so we, though many, are one body in Christ, and individually members one of another.
—Romans 12:5

Memories are links in a golden chain that bind us until we meet again.
—Jacqueline Winspear

Sample Prayer

Lord, I am anxious with so much to do on my visit, and I do not know what to expect. Please calm my soul, help me prioritize my time, and honor those I visit. Help me to reflect you to those I meet and provide me with loving boldness with my unbelieving friends and family. I need a renewed vision for how you will use me when I return. Please refresh my zeal to serve you and give me rest.

Disclaimer

My views and opinions are my own and may or may not align with any entity with which I am now or have been affiliated. They may also not align with your sending agency, fellowship, or company.

Additional Resources

Young, Amy, *Looming Transitions*

Notes

Notes

CHAPTER NINE

RETURNING

Leaving a Host Country with No Plans to Move Back

For everything there is a season, and a time for every matter under heaven …
—Ecclesiastes 3:1

Only one life, 'twill soon be past, only what's done for Christ will last.
—C. T. Studd

When the time comes to depart your host country, either to change counties or return to your passport country, invite counsel early!

Meet with your organization, sending fellowship, or other "parent" organization well before you plan to return. This is respectful to them and, in most cases, will help you work through logistics and reveal transition issues you might otherwise overlook, like changes to insurance or moving expenses. A healthy transition is vital for you to become a positive contributor in your next role.

If your host country has been your home for many years, your passport country may be foreign and unfamiliar. For parents, moving to your "home" country will be like your original move to your host country for your children—ask the Lord for extra insights, patience, and grace with them.

Read the "Preparing" and "Leaving" chapters in Part One for helpful tips and follow the same timelines.

For this chapter, I take the perspective that you have been away from your passport country for at least two years.

Guiding Principles

- Practice good goodbyes and build your RAFT.
- **Check your motives.** Confirm you are following God, not pursuing ease or running away from something. Discuss your plans honestly and transparently with trusted friends, mentors, church leaders, and counselors. Your returning story can be a testimony to God's providence and provision or a regret that haunts your future.
- Returning does not mean you have failed—in most cases.
- Work though the "Discerning," "Leaving," and "Packing" chapters.

Indicators That it May Be Time to Leave

Is it **time to return?**

We lived in the Middle East/North Africa region, where one is served "**goodbye coffee**" when the host is ready for you to leave. What **indicators** do you see that it is time to leave your host country?

There is a natural ending.
- You joined a team for a fixed period, which has ended.
- You **complete the project** you were sent to do.
- Your **team disbands.**
- Your **contract ends.**
- Those you support leave.

Family dynamics change.

- Your **mental or physical health deteriorates** and treatment is not available in your context.
    - A change of venue may or may not alleviate your issues.
    - Determine the **root causes**.
- **Aging parents** require care.
    - You may be **the best or only option** to support them.
    - Or, you may appear to be the best, but not be!
    - **Seek wise counsel!**
    - Many will quote Matthew 19:29: "And everyone who has left houses or brothers or sisters or father or mother or children or lands, for my name's sake, will receive a hundredfold and will inherit eternal life."
    - **Do not forget 1 Timothy 5:8**: "But if anyone does not provide for his relatives, and especially for members of his household, he has denied the faith and is worse than an unbeliever."
- **Children have needs** that you cannot meet in your current context.
    - Differentiate **needs versus preferences**.
    - Seek guidance from medical and other professionals, plus parents whose children have similar needs and understand your context.
    - Parenting involves sacrifice, and may include laying down your dreams of cross-cultural ministry to provide for your child's needs, at least temporarily.

Do not overstay your welcome!

- **You are not irreplaceable.**
    - If you think you are, you are probably either **burned out** or headed there.
- You do not get bonus points for staying while your life is imploding, the health of aging parents is declining, or children are failing socially or academically, or any combination thereof.

○ Delay while your mental or physical health deteriorates will **take resources and undermine** your team's work and negatively impact your ministry partners.

Making the Decision

This is a **weighty decision.**

- **A discernment retreat** is an excellent first step.
  - ○ Take some time where you can drown out competing voices to focus on listening to the Lord.
  - ○ Evaluate what works and does not in your current context, and what would or not work in a new place.
  - ○ Honestly evaluate your gifts and skills.
- **Do not decide alone.**
  - ○ Invite others to pray for you during your discernment retreat.
  - ○ Ask close friends, mature spiritual leaders, your member care department, and your sending pastor or other church representative to help you **evaluate your decision.**
  - ○ Include medical and other professionals as necessary.
- Read the third section of *Grit to Stay Grace to Go* by Sue Eenigenburg and Eva Burkholder to help you work through less obvious decisions.
- Sometimes the decision is not up to you.
  - ○ See the "Unplanned Departures" section below.

Beware of idolatry!

- Prioritize your **identity as a child of God**, a spouse, a child of your earthly parents, or a parent over your identity as a cross-cultural ministry worker.
- **Unwillingness to leave** may indicate that your mission has become an idol.

———— Communicate your Plans ————

Your supporters have supported you through your international work, whether prayerfully, financially, or as a friend. They deserve to know what, why, and when.

Avoid surprises!
- **Ask supporters to join you in prayer for direction**, even as you discern your next steps.
  - Some may drop support, but most will stay and appreciate your honesty.
- Once you decide, **notify your supporters as soon as possible**, including how you arrived at your decision.
- **Ask for help** with your return.
  - Most consider it an honor to help you as part of their contribution to the kingdom.
  - Ask well in advance, from a home to stay in while you settle in to borrowing a car.

———— Prepare Emotionally ————

You may depart after your initial term, your initial month, after several terms, with a walker, or in a pine box. If you depart before you planned to, know it is not before Our Father planned (if you are walking in obedience to him).

Leave well.
- **Say "goodbye"** to friends and special places.
- Build your RAFT. (See the "Leaving" chapter for more details.)
- In your final two months, **assume each goodbye is your last.**
  - Some friends may travel before you leave, but return after you leave.
- **Do not promise to return**—even definite plans are subject to change.
- **Give plenty of notice** to your landlord, children's school, language center, and other places dependent on you for income.

Schedule time to rest and adjust.

- Many are inclined to "jump right in," and virtually all of them regret it.
- If possible, give yourself a few months to readjust.

Prepare to be disoriented.

- **You have changed.**
- The home you left **has changed** (even if the GPS coordinates are close).
- **Friends and family have changed.**
  - They have moved on or moved away.
- The city to which you return may not be the one you left.
- If your time away has been long, or your passport country has gone through significant social and/or political change, your experience may be more like moving to a new culture than you realize.
  - Even after only six months, you will recognize changes.
  - Prepare yourself for reverse culture shock.
- Most **friends, colleagues, and strangers do not understand** your work or your life abroad, nor can they fully grasp your experiences.
  - **Be patient** with them.

Making new friends may be more difficult than you expect.

- Cross-cultural workers, especially in ministry, have often enjoyed a greater depth of community and common purpose than they find on their return.
- You and, if you are parents, your child(ren), may be accustomed to making new friends quickly and going "deep" early in your relationship, which may be quite foreign in your passport country or new location.

Lighten up—be prepared to be a foreigner in your passport country.

- When you say something wrong or cannot remember a word, laugh it off.
- Find the humor in your fiascos—which will also give you fun stories to share with others.

Resume your "learner" attitude.
- You may be a learner longer than you expect!
- If you return to your "home country," you need time to adjust to what it has become.
- If you move to a new country, you are back to the "Arriving" chapter.
- **Give yourself grace.**

Prepare for questions, including ignorant or offensive ones.
- Most people honestly **cannot imagine the life you lived abroad.**
  - Take Jesus's approach when he said, "… forgive them, for they know not what they do …" (Luke 23:34)
- Give God the glory by sharing how he sanctified and used you.
- **Give God-honoring answers to offensive questions.** Some you might hear:
  - "How was your trip?" though you were away for years.
  - "Are you happy to be home?" when that place no longer feels like home, or you move to a new city.
  - "Aren't you happy to be here where it is safe?" though you may have been safer where you were.
  - "What is it like to be a failed missionary?" This one requires the grace of the Heavenly Father to answer.

Schedule counseling sessions before your departure if needed.
- Someone you can connect with in person after you arrive.

If your departure was due to team dysfunction.
- Schedule time to work through this with your sending fellowship and/or organization.
- You may need a third party to help resolve issues or concerns.
  - If the other party will not engage, you may need additional counseling to recover.
- Own your part of the dysfunction.

Prepare Professionally

Start looking for your next job six months or longer before your departure, if possible.

- Start the process, but **give yourself time to reconnect and settle** before you start your new role.
  - An extended period displays a lack of initiative.
  - Start your search in earnest within a month or two of returning.
- Realistically evaluate your skills, your capacity, and your timeline for re-entry.
  - Do you need to take courses or otherwise improve or update your skills?
  - Determine **what you like to do**, not just what you can do.
- Depending on your time away and expertise before you left, you may "start over" when you return.
  - If you plan to change your work (ministry to industry, or vice versa), a career coach can help you update your resume and help you sell your skills

Transfer your tasks and/or projects.

- Find a **local partner you can empower** to replace you, if possible.
- **Distribute or eliminate** remaining workload.
  - Work with your team and team leader to determine distribution.
  - Prepare yourself for some of your work to end.
  - A healthy team should not simply increase the workload of others because a member leaves.
  - This does not mean the work you did was without value, but that others either lack the necessary skills or other work has a higher priority.

Retiring?

- **No one retires** from God's service—you just change your mission field.
- **Meet with your financial planner** at least six months before departure.
- **Invest in others serving cross-culturally** or on that path.

- Write a book (even if only for friends and family), consolidate your newsletters into a folder, or create a photo album to memorialize your experience.

Returning is Costly

Beyond the obvious costs of setting up your household and acquiring transportation when returning to one's home country or moving to a new country, there are hidden costs.

- Most who return from the mission field **miss the intimacy they had with their team.**
- People in your passport country cannot understand the life you lived abroad.
  - Recognize that only you and those who were with you understand who you were and bring that into who you are.
  - You will feel a loss of "that part of you" that lived and ministered abroad.
    - Grieve that loss.
- Plan to be lonely and misunderstood until you establish your "new you" in your new context.

Unplanned Departures

Sometimes a visa is not renewed—you return to your host country and are not allowed to enter. Anecdote: One friend took his family to their passport country for two weeks, during which time their host country expelled all the expatriates and they were never allowed to return, not even to gather their things.

- Work with your sending organization or company and sending fellowship as soon as possible to **determine your options.**
- **Share specific needs** with your supporters and prayer partners, material and otherwise.
- **Debrief.**

- ○ Grieving these unresolved losses may be more difficult than you expect.
- ○ Not grieving these losses will impact you negatively in the future.

Leaving a dysfunctional team,
- • Work with your sending fellowship or organization about the failure in order to prevent future problems, or reveal mistakes you made, and
- • Read *Bully Pulpit* for more thoughts on the topic of toxic leadership, including what is toxic vs. what you just do not like.

Logistics

— In Your Host Country —

Ending your lease or selling your home.
- • Determine **what is expected** well in advance, and compare notes with others who left before you to determine what is reasonable.
  - ○ A new coat of paint, repairs, and returning your place to the state it was in when you arrived are all reasonable requests.

Arrange for final bills to be paid (utility, etc.).

— In Your New or Passport Country —

Make temporary arrangements.
- • Organize **a place to stay** upon your return well before you leave, if possible.
  - ○ Plan for several months.
- • **Arrange for a car** for a month or so.
  - ○ If you will purchase a vehicle, this gives you time to look.

Review the "Leaving" and "Packing" chapters.
- • Confirm your baggage counts and prepare to pay for excess baggage if necessary.
- • If you have a long-term visa, determine what is required to cancel it.

Debrief, ideally a month or two after you have returned and begun to settle in.

- Plan on **at least a week.**
- If possible, attend a **residential debriefing**.
- Debriefs give you an opportunity to share your story with someone who understands and is trained to listen, which most in your passport country do not and are not.
- Your debrief should also help you understand loss and stages of grief.
  - If not, find a resource to help you work through these.
- The book *Returning Well* by Melissa Chaplin is a self-directed, long-term debriefing tool (six weeks to six months at your discretion) that would be a good addition to an in-person, several-day debrief.
- Your debrief may surface areas that you need to work through in **counseling**.

Do you need a new church?

- Some return without a "home church."
  - Before you leave, start to research new churches.
  - You **need fellowship and feeding**.
- Some return without a "sending church."
  - Reach out to missional churches.
  - Share what you have to offer:
    - Will you host or coordinate short-term teams?
    - Offer to help with their missions program.
    - Seek first what you can give, not what you can get.
  - Be honest if you need financial support, but ensure that is not the sole purpose for your conversation.
  - Ask for oversight and care, and determine if they are prepared to provide it.
  - Read the "Sending" chapter to learn more about what to look for in a sending church.

Encouragement

Your departure may make you sad, glad, relieved, disappointed, depressed, or some or all of those. This is normal. Even if you leave a robust ministry which you started or supported, leaving may feel like you failed. You are not alone.

You may feel disloyal to local friends when you have to leave an untenable situation, and find it unjust that you have options that they do not. You may feel guilty that you are excited to leave, and your grace for what you do not like may fade long before you go. Anecdote: We still hear the voices of locals we love asking why we had to leave—and why we could not take them with us.

Multi-day debriefing will help you process your loss and grief, to work through hidden losses you may not realize.

God's plans for you are perfect. His timing for your work is ideal, though you may not agree in the moment. Your time in the field has developed you on his timeline, sanctified you according to his plans, and prepared you for what he has for you next.

The steps of a man are established by the LORD, when he delights in his way …
—Psalm 27:23

God is most glorified in us when we are most satisfied in Him.
—John Piper

Sample Prayer

Lord, I am confused. I am willing to follow anywhere you lead me, but this chapter is closing. I face another term of uncertainty and discomfort. Please preserve my joy in you alone and help me glorify you by my satisfaction in you. Please go before me in this transition, so that I can honor you in my next position, home, and community.

Disclaimer

My views and opinions are my own and may or may not align with any entity with which I am now or have been affiliated. They may also not align with your sending agency, fellowship, or company.

Additional Resources

Chaplin, Melissa, *Returning Well*

Eenigenburg, Sue and Eva Burkholder, *Grit to Stay Grace to Go*

Young, Amy, *Looming Transitions*

Notes

Notes

PART TWO

TOPICAL INFORMATION AND ADVICE

CHAPTER TEN

SELF-CARE

But the Lord answered her, "Martha, Martha, you are anxious and troubled about many things, but one thing is necessary. Mary has chosen the good portion, which will not be taken away from her."

—Luke 10:41–42

My hope is built on nothing less than Jesus Christ, my righteousness; I dare not trust the sweetest frame, But wholly lean on Jesus' name.

—Edward Mote,
"My Hope is Built on Nothing Less"

Too often I have heard "someone should have," when the reality is that the "someone" is the speaker! "Someone should have known …," yet the speaker did their best to hide whatever it was. The West seems to have succumbed to an everything-is-someone-else's-problem-to-solve mentality, which has crept into mission work.

The most important takeaway from this chapter is that **you are responsible for your care.** Do not wait for someone to come to you.

If you are not ready to take ownership of developing a proactive plan to maintain and, if necessary, restore your physical and mental health, you need to remain in or return to a place where you can receive adequate professional care with the support of family and friends. Those who do not become a burden to their team and undermine their team's ability to fulfill their vision and goals.

See additional content in the following chapters on "Singleness", "Marriage", and "Parenting."

Guiding Principles

- You are responsible for your care.
- Build and maintain your network of carers with regular contact.
- Raise your hand early when you need help.

Be Proactive

You are responsible for your care, including:
- Your **relationship with God**,
- Your **physical and mental wellbeing**,
- Your **language and culture acquisition** at a pace that is aggressive, but sustainable, and the
- **Development and maintenance of friendships** on and off your team.

Raise your hand—early!
- **No one knows what you need if you do not ask** for help.
  - If you allow your **physical or mental health to deteriorate, you become an avoidable burden** on your team, organization, and sending fellowship!
- Do not wait for "someone" to contact you.

Deepen your theological foundation.
- Find others to **study a systematic theology book** together.
- Develop a **robust theology of suffering.**

- Listen to theologically sound **sermons**.

Grieve your losses.
- You will experience **physical losses** (favorite foods or drinks, face-to-face time with lifelong friends, your health, or sleep) and **intangible losses** (sense of accomplishment, sense of belonging, respect related to prior accomplishments).
    - Acknowledge and grieve these losses to help you work through them.
    - Regular debriefing will help.

Do not compare.
- People have different capacities for language, work, and physical activity.
- If you are over stretched due to "common expectations" by your team leader, discuss your needs and change teams if necessary.

Tips to Stay Healthy

Pray.
- Your time with God is the best way to build the resilience, patience, mental fortitude, and correct outlook to flourish on the field (or anywhere).
- Give God your fears, anxious thoughts, frustrations, and future.

Read.
- Study Scripture.
- Mix up reading fast for the general theme and slow to understand each passage.

Rest.
- Continue (or start) **sabbath** rests.
- With your tithe, you trust God with your money.
    - With your sabbath, you **trust him with your time.**

Maintain your advocacy team.
- See the "Preparing" chapter in Part One for more details.

- Communicate with them regularly.
- Let them help you get medications or other needed items to you.
  - Plan months ahead to allow for delays and canceled trips.

Have fun.
- Enjoy or develop (then enjoy) **a hobby.**
  - **Do something you love** every day, even for a few minutes.
  - Be sensitive to local norms.
  - For example, sunbathing for a woman in a conservative Muslim culture might not be the best hobby choice.

Debrief.
- Enroll in a multi-day debrief **after your first six months** on the field, then just before or after your **first home leave**/furlough, and then **every two to four years, after changing countries, or changing teams.**
  - Expect to spend **three to five days.**
  - It sounds like a long commitment, but it takes that long to fully process your experience.
  - If you have children older than six, find a family debriefing.
- One purpose is to "**empty the barrel**" (from the Le Rucher Ministries debrief training) regularly to keep little problems from accumulating into bigger problems.
  - This is not the same as a **trauma** or **crisis debrief.**
- Visit DHarakalAuthor.org for a list of up-to-date debriefing centers.

Leave your host country regularly if it is spiritually, physically, or emotionally stressful.
- Changing contexts helps with resiliency and perspective.
- **Every three to six months** is a good timeframe.
  - Some visas require this.
- If you live in near-constant strain, these breaks are particularly important.
- If you live in a comfortable environment, still **visit another region** of the country where you can relax and get away from your daily work.

- Vacations are important in all fields, not just ministry—and getting away is more psychologically and emotionally refreshing for most people.

Attend important family events.
- You will miss many smaller events (birthdays, graduations), but do not miss the biggest ones, which include, but are not limited to:
    - Marriage of immediate family member, maybe best friend
    - First child born to or adopted by a sibling
    - Death of immediate family member

Prevent scope creep for you and others.
- As a team, **determine what can be left undone.**
    - Not everything that has been done must continue.
- What can you **turn over to local partners?**
    - Give them ownership—trust your partners.
- **Survey** beneficiaries *and* team members to determine the highest-value work for each.

Circles of Care

Build (and maintain) your support network.
- **God must be your most intimate and frequent contact,** the center of your circles.
    - Follow King David's model from the Psalms—pour your heart out to him.
- **Then close friends or peers** who can maintain confidentiality.
    - This would include your advocacy team.
- **Your member care and pastoral support** are probably more reactive than proactive.
    - If they do not contact you regularly (at least every three to four months), contact them.

- This is the layer where your organization's or sending fellowship's member care department resides.
  - Do you know your assigned member care person?
  - When did you last communicate with them?
- Last is the **professional layer**.
  - These are your professional counselors, medical professionals, psychologists, et cetera.
- Images like this one abound.
  - This is one I cobbled together.
  - Do you have someone for every layer?
  - See the **Self-Care Contact List** in the appendix.

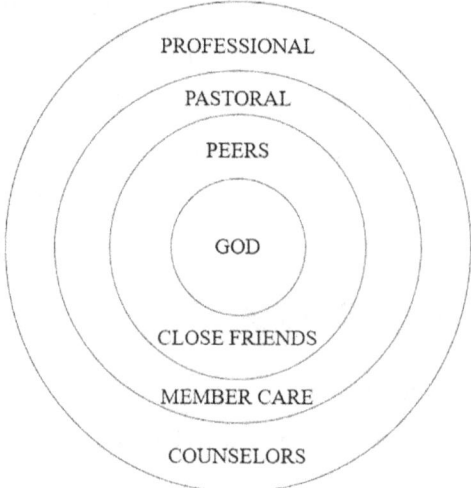

Team Care

Some teams are supported by large organizations with member care functions. Some are not. In either case, you need team-level care.

- Someone on the team needs to check in.
  - Do you have someone in each level, and do you meet with them as often as you plan to?

- That "someone" does not need to be the leader.
  - The leader may be the least available given their responsibilities.
  - Is there a person on the team who has a heart for care?
  - If not, as this is primarily checking in, the role can be rotated, under the leader's guidance.
- That "someone" needs to have the rest of their responsibilities adjusted.
  - This cannot be part of scope creep.

Encouragement

My father taught me it is easier to stay well than to get well. Build your care network, use it, and maintain it, to remain healthy and model health for others. This allows you to be a resource for your team, not a burden. Weigh more heavily what you can offer than what you can take, and make frequent, intimate time for the Lord who loves you.

People want to help you, but they cannot if you do not ask. We live in the Middle East/North Africa region and minor upset stomachs are common. It is also quite dusty all summer, which leads to allergies (for me). View these minor things as minor things—do not blow them out of proportion or, as my dad said, "Don't make mountains out of molehills."

Self-care is most beneficial when you are proactive and treat ailments or stressors when they are small.

Do not be conformed to this world, but be transformed by the renewal of your mind, that by testing you may discern what is the will of God, what is good and acceptable and perfect.
—Romans 12:2

I believe that the greatest gift you can give your family and the world is a healthy you.
—Joyce Meyer

Sample Prayer

Lord, please protect my mind, body, soul, and spirit. Great Physician, show me those people who can help me to maintain or restore my health so that I can fulfill the purposes to which you called me. Please let my life reflect Psalm 73:25b, "… and there is nothing on earth that I desire besides you."

Please lead me to those who will turn me back to you when I am dissatisfied and protect me from those who would encourage my complaining.

Disclaimer

My views and opinions are my own and may or may not align with any entity with which I am now or have been affiliated. They may also not align with your sending agency, fellowship, or company. Further, I am not a counselor.

Additional Resources

Alma, Carissa, *Thriving in Cross-Cultural Ministry*

Haidt, Jonathan, *The Anxious Generation (Parenting)*

Kruger, Michael J., *Bully Pulpit*

The Austin Stone *Hour of Prayer* (*www.austinstone.org/videos/hour-of-prayer*)

Notes

Notes

CHAPTER ELEVEN

CONTRACTING

Memorandums of Understanding (MOUs)

Come now, let us make a covenant, you and I. And let it be a witness between you and me.

—Genesis 31:44

Good fences make good neighbors.

—Robert Frost

You need some kind of governance document. Being "led by the Spirit" and "trusting people to know what they need to do" are well and good—until someone (or you) breaks an unwritten team rule or misses an undocumented expectation.

Read all governing documents and policies thoroughly before you commit to a team. If there are non-negotiable elements that are important to you and the leader is unwilling to adapt, you should look for a new team.

Guiding Principles

- An MOU must set discrete expectations and establish a clear vision.
- Any understanding you have not documented in your MOU is not an agreement.
- If you have "non-negotiables," these must be included in the MOU or an addendum, signed by you and your team leader. Negotiate matters important to your health and flourishing on the field (e.g., visiting sick parents, attending a sibling's wedding or other expected or unexpected

---

What is an MOU?

From Dictionary.com: A Memorandum of Understanding (MOU) is "a document that describes the general principles of an agreement between parties, but does not amount to a substantive contract." An MOU sets forth expectations for leaders and team members, is typically written by an organization or team leader and, unlike a contract, is not legally binding. Clear, written expectations help avoid misunderstandings and the resulting tension or animosity.

Talk to people on the team. If they are unfamiliar with the MOU, that is a warning that the team does not follow it, which sounds empowering, but is more often frustrating when you are unsure of boundaries.

This information and sample MOU are based on my own experience plus MOUs I received from a number of different organizations for review.

Elements of an Effective MOU

An MOU should contain enough detail to establish clear expectations with enough flexibility to adapt to your specific gifts and goals. The following elements **should be concise and clear.**

Team Vision
- "Where there is no vision, the people perish …" (Proverbs 29:18a KJV)
- Your team's vision is the guiding concept to the MOU.
- **Ensure you share the team's vision.**
  - If you join a team with a different vision than yours, you may become quite frustrated.

Team Roles and Leadership Structure
- Is the team hierarchical or is leadership shared?
- Does everyone on the team have the same role, or can each person express their gifts and learn about others?
- Is there a clear decision-maker?
  - Shared decision-making sounds great, but can be quite frustrating when a decision needs to be made quickly.

Commitments
- Look for **commitments for leaders and participants.**
- Team leaders and participants should share in some commitments (e.g., committed response times) and differ in others (e.g., daily routine).
- It should concern you if all the documented commitments are for team members with nothing for leaders.

Time Expectations
- New team members often have more of their days structured based on the wisdom and experience of the leaders and language requirements.
- If you expect some autonomy, but the week is fully scheduled, you have a disconnect.
  - Discuss with your team leader.
- How do others on the team spend their days?
  - Does the MOU reflect their answers?

Team Rhythms

- How much time dedicated each week/month is reserved for **team activities?**
- What are the attendance and absence policies?

Travel Policy

- Are there restrictions on when or where you travel?
- Are there expectations to leave the country (e.g., visa runs, annual extended stay out of the host country)?
- It is not uncommon for one's first home leave to be a few years after their initial deployment.

Decision Matrix

- The MOU should spell out specifically **what requires approval versus notification.**
- For approvals, the decision maker and the time required for the decision should be spelled out specifically.
  - For example, you may be allowed to take a visa run within certain parameters, but still need to notify your team leader and/or sending organization.
  - To miss a team meeting (except for illness) might require approval.

Conflict Resolution Process

- Teams are built with flawed humans.
- **Conflicts will arise.**
  - What is the conflict resolution process?

Communication Protocols

- What communication tools does the team use for different information?
- What are the **expected response times?**
  - Do team members and leaders honor them in practice?

Agreement

- If there are elements in the MOU with which you disagree, or if it is silent on a point important to you, discuss with your team leader.
  - **Document agreed-to exceptions in the MOU** before either you or your team leader signs it.
  - If your team leader is unwilling to adjust the MOU, this may not be the team for you. Seek wise counsel.
- **Verbal agreements are not agreements.**

Encouragement

Those who give up the comforts of home to move to a place that is unknown and foreign rarely crave rules and structure, but that is exactly what you and your team need. For such expectations, Brené Brown captured the need well: "Clear is kind. Unclear is unkind."

I have worked with many frustrated team members who have been corrected for breaking unwritten rules because "you should have known." The MOU is the place to kindly create the clarity needed to avoid that scenario. It should be long enough to express mutual expectations clearly, but short enough that it does not require a Pharisee to interpret it. An effective MOU is a document to help you understand the safe boundaries within which you can roam freely.

Let each of you look not only to his own interests, but also to the interests of others.
—Philippians 2:4

Unless both sides win, no agreement can be permanent.
—Jimmy Carter

Sample Prayer

Lord, I do not like to be restricted. I know you are a God of order, and that you have placed me under authority for my good. Please give me joy in structure and peace in the safety that good boundaries provide. Help me be gracious and wise when there are discrepancies to resolve.

Disclaimer

My views and opinions are my own and may or may not align with any entity with which I am now or have been affiliated. They may also not align with your sending agency, fellowship, or company.

Additional Resources

Find an MOU template at www.DHarakalAuthor.org.

---- **Notes** ----

Notes

CHAPTER TWELVE

PACKING

And my God will supply every need of yours according to his riches in glory in Christ Jesus.
—Philippians 4:19

I get ideas about what's essential when packing my suitcase.
—Diane von Furstenberg

Moving to a new culture is a herculean task. My wife and I have moved internationally three times. First, with a huge multi-national company. Second, we moved from the U.S. to the Middle East with just what we could check on our flight. Third was our most recent move between two Middle Eastern countries complete with damage and insurance claims.

The following recommendations assume you plan to live comfortably—not extravagantly nor impoverished. The suggestions are geared towards those who will move with what can be checked on flights—including the option to pay for additional checked bags.

When we moved to the Middle East/North Africa region from the United States the two of us had eight checked bags—two hard-sided roller bags, four tubs, and two duffel bags. That may sound excessive or insufficient. Some move with one checked bag; others need a twenty-foot container. What is right for you is between you, your sending organization, and your receiving team.

For an editable packing list including links, visit www.DHarakalAuthor.org.

Guiding Principles

- Take what is necessary, special, or comforting, realizing any item may be lost.
- Align with your receiving team.
- Ensure any necessary medications are available in your new country or pack enough to last until you can get more, plus an extra month.

General Suggestions

Talk to your receiving team.
- Get their suggestions for **what to take and what to leave.**
- If they do not have a document, and they onboard new members with any frequency, create one and send it back for validation to **create a resource for future team members.**

How to decide **what to take and what to leave.**
- One suggestion is to **take what you love**, what is **necessary**, and what is **comforting.**
- **Leave bulky**, inexpensive items available in your new country.
- When is your first **"restocking"** opportunity?
  - Can you wait for friends, family, or others to bring you items when they visit?
- **Take a power bank** that will fit in your purse/pocket (one per person).
- **Be prepared to lose anything you take.**
  - Unexpected expulsions or visa denials happen.

––––––––––––––––––––– **What to Pack** –––––––––––––––––––––

Where you move will impact what you need to take.

We had few choices in our first Middle Eastern country, and what was available was expensive. Our next home city had an IKEA and many stores that carried our favorite American and European products. Some countries have healthy online retailers and efficient delivery. These will impact what you need to take.

Share this list with your receiving team to get their advice if they do not have a list of their own.

You may still want to take some of your favorite items and refills.

Items I found most necessary are in bold.

Electronics

If the voltage in your host country is different from your passport country, ensure any electronics you take are dual voltage.

☐ **Cell phone power bank** per person

☐ **Universal travel plug adapter**

☐ Noise-canceling headphones (for language)

☐ Bluetooth speaker

☐ Computer/phone and charging cords

☐ Adapter to connect your phone or computer to a television

☐ E-reader (physical books take up space and weight)

☐ Small cloud-based voice-activated speaker or device

Leave behind large items and those with a different voltage that are not dual-voltage.

Kitchen

☐ Favorite specialty items

☐ Favorite chef's knife

☐ Specialty coffee equipment

☐ Oven thermometer

☐ Specific items/spices not available in your host country

Leave behind most pots, pans, and basic kitchen tools available in your new location.

Bedroom & linens

- ☐ Your favorite pillow
- ☐ Bedding, if it will make your new place feel like home
- ☐ Fitted sheets (if unavailable in your new country)
- ☐ Top sheets (if unavailable in your new country)

Leave most bedding.

Bathroom & toiletries

- ☐ **Basic toiletries** for your first few weeks
- ☐ Specific toiletries important to you (hair products, skincare, makeup)
- ☐ Shower filter and refills (if recommended)

Leave non-essential items.

Health

- ☐ **Basic first aid kit**
- ☐ **Digital copies of your medical and dental records** for your doctors in your new country
- ☐ At least **one-month supply of required medications** (even if available locally)
- ☐ At least **six months' supply** or more of medications not available in your host country
- ☐ Preferred **over-the-counter medications** not available in your new city
- ☐ **Vitamins** you take or plan to take
- ☐ Small specialty exercise equipment
- ☐ Glasses (two pairs) & contacts with updated prescription

Ensure your prescription medications are in their original containers.

Clothing

- ☐ **Culturally appropriate wardrobe**
  - ○ If you need to purchase new clothing, can you buy it locally after you arrive to ensure appropriateness, and get to know your new country?

- ○ If the idea of shopping in your new country causes stress, shop before you leave.
  - ○ Ensure you plan your budget accordingly.
- ☐ **Warm house slippers** (even in warm climates if floors are cold)
- ☐ **Good rain gear**, including shoes, even for desert climates
- ☐ Other comfortable clothing for visa runs (e.g., shorts, T-shirts, bathing suit)
- ☐ Avoid taking too much clothing or too many shoes unless your platform involves fashion modeling
- ☐ For families, especially with small children, clothing a size or two larger

Leave old, worn-out clothes.

Documents (both physical and digital copies)
- ☐ **Copies of wills and powers of attorney** (PoA) (originals should be with the executor and person delegated as PoA, respectively)
- ☐ **Certified Birth Certificate**(s)
- ☐ **Certified Marriage Certificate**
- ☐ **Shot/immunization records.** (Some countries require an International Certification of Vaccination wwwnc.cdc.gov/travel/page/icvp).
- ☐ **Driver's licenses**
- ☐ For adopted children, the adoption decree

Miscellaneous
- ☐ **Luggage scale**
- ☐ A few items that remind you of home (e.g., photos of favorite people or places)
- ☐ Items for your **hobby** (e.g., guitar, craft supplies, hiking boots, favorite kitchen items)
- ☐ **Favorite Bible** (if allowed in your host country)
- ☐ Favorite journal and a few extras
- ☐ A few favorite books

Leave non-favorite, non-essential, bulky items.

Digital Suggestions

☐ **Scan medical records:** drug prescriptions, home-country doctor info, eyeglass prescriptions, etc.

☐ **Document important records** and share with someone in your home country.

☐ **Leave signed, original** <u>will</u> with your executor.

☐ **Leave signed, original** <u>power of attorney, durable power of attorney, and medical power of attorney</u> with your agent/attorney-in-fact.

☐ **Establish a remote backup service** for your computers, tablets, and phones, and backup at least weekly, starting a few weeks before you depart.

☐ **Get an encrypted drive** if you cannot do cloud backup from your host country.

☐ **Photograph special objects** that you will not take.

☐ Digitize original art and print a copy to take with you.

☐ Set up an electronic picture frame if you want to keep up with photos of family and friends.

Plan ahead. These documents may take time to gather and photograph or scan.

How to Pack

These are ideas, tips, and tricks I have learned after traveling over two million miles to a few dozen countries, plus what others have shared with me. This is a lot of information. Read through it quickly and then take each piece when you are ready.

— General Suggestions —

Plan ahead.

- **Pack over time.**
  - You do not want to run to the airport with no sleep because you packed all night before your flight.
- Allocate at least a full day to pack.

- It will take longer than you expect, and **you will need to redistribute weight**.

Buy **nesting suitcases**.
- Purchase a matching carry-on for each additional family member, where appropriate.
- **Hard-sided** will wear better than soft-sided.
- Why nesting? Your storage space may be limited in your new place.
  - Gives you different size options for trips while you are abroad.
- **Good luggage is not cheap. Cheap luggage is not good.**
- **Avoid black luggage** and try to buy the same color.
  - This makes it easier to identify in baggage claim.

Use some large **duffel bags.**
- Great for bedding, clothing, and anything vacuum-packed.
- They take up little space when you unpack and offer a great weight-to-capacity ratio.
- **Pack a lightweight duffel bag** (large or small) that folds into a small footprint.
  - Handy if you need to repack at the airport or buy things during travel and need more space.

Tubs work well.
- Confirm that they comply with airline size requirements.
- Use for well-wrapped fragile items, boxes, and things with corners that might tear a duffel bag.
- **Zip tie all four corners** and tape 6–8 extra zip ties on the top. If customs opens them, they can re-secure the lids.
- **Write your contact info on the inside and outside with a permanent** marker.
  - Include your last name, personal email address (not organization), and phone number.
  - Do not include a physical address.

- They can provide storage in your new home or stack in less space than several large suitcases.

Get matching, durable **luggage tags.**
- Buy tags that are easily recognizable, will hide your information, and will not tear off your bag.
- Include your name, email, and phone only (with country code), not an address.

Use **two brightly colored luggage straps per bag.**
- One from top to bottom, and one around the middle.
- Protects against failed zippers/clasps.
- **Using the same color** helps with identification.
- Write **only your name, phone number, and email address** on them in case your primary name tags are lost.

Use **TSA-approved locks** for bags without built-in locks.
- Have them for your carry-on bag as well, in case you have to check it.

Pack everything a week before you leave (two weeks is better).
- Including your carry-on bags, to make sure you have space, time to get last-minute items, and stay within weight limits.
- Use a **luggage scale** and know the airline limits to avoid unexpected fees.
    - Weigh with **luggage straps and locks** on your bags.
    - Keep your bag a pound/half Kg **under the allowable weight** as airport scales may weigh differently, and some airlines are sticklers.
- Lock all but one or two of your bags (as few as possible).
    - **Live out of your unlocked bag(s) and your carry-on bag(s)** for your final days or weeks, so your major packing is out of the way and you can spend your final days with friends and family.

— *Packing Your Carry-On Bag(s)* —

As you pack your carry-on bag(s), consider what you might need if all of your checked luggage was lost for several days.

- **Important documents** (see above)
- Energy bars/snacks for unexpected delays
- A water bottle to fill after security (flights are dehydrating)
- Toiletries in a TSA-approved clear bag
  - A heavy-duty clear bag with a zipper will outlast a Ziplock-style bag.
- Small first aid kit, including medications you might need for the first few months (pain reliever, antiacid, etc.)—check with your receiving team
- Clothes for two days, including sleepwear
- All of your electronics, jewelry, and cash. Do not put these in your checked luggage.
- Your luggage scale.
  - You will need it up to the very end and it takes up little space.
- Something light and small that will make you feel "at home": photographs, small painting, etc.

Pack an age-appropriate bag for each child.
- **Keep the weight light.**
- Ensure it will **strap to your bag** when they tire of carrying or rolling it.
- If they wait to open it until after you take off, it helps them think through the stages of travel.
  - **Ideas for young children:** Inexpensive new toys and special snacks for each flight, Band-Aids, things to draw or color, a small pack of new crayons or colored pencils, books with reusable stickers, but nothing loud or electronic without **headphones** which your child is accustomed to wearing.
  - You do not want to pack bulky headphones only to find out your child will not wear them.

— *Packing your Checked Luggage* —

Mix clothes in different checked bags.
- If one bag is lost, you are not completely without clothing.
- If traveling as a couple or family, put sets of clothes for each person in each checked bag.

Wrap fragile items in T-shirts, socks, etc., and put them in a Ziploc-style bag in case they do break.

Do not pack items empty—put socks or other small items inside of shoes, etc.

Use vacuum bags and two- to three-gallon Ziploc-style bags
- **Warning:** vacuum-packed items take up less space but get denser, so the same volume in a suitcase weighs much more.
  - Duffel bags are good for vacuum-packed items.
  - Mix with other items that are not dense—a large duffel bag or Tote-a-Ton packed exclusively with vacuum-packed items will probably **exceed airline weight limits**.
- Plastic bags **keep items dry** in case your bag sits on the tarmac in a downpour.
  - Moist, smelly, ruined items make for an unpleasant start to your life away.
- If your zipper or clasp fails, these also prevent your items from spilling out onto the conveyor belt.
- You will use more than you think you will need, so leave time to get extras or buy more than you need with time to return what you do not use.
- One or two extra-large vacuum bags will help if you plan to take comforters, bedspreads, and pillows.
- Put everything else in medium and large bags (the small ones are not that useful).
- **Leave a little air** so they are not rock hard. This makes them easier to pack.

Put **liquids in Ziploc-style freezer bags.**

- Unscrew the lids, **put plastic over the mouth**, then screw the lid back on.
- You can also wrap tape around the cap.
- In both cases, still pack in a plastic zipper storage bag.

Pack special notes or cards in a freezer bag to help with homesickness.

Pack a **good first aid kit** for your home.

- Visit the Red Cross website at www.redcross.org/get-help/how-to-prepare-for-emergencies/anatomy-of-a-first-aid-kit.html

Document what is in each bag.

- If one is lost or delayed, you will know what you are missing.

--------- **Encouragement** ---------

If you try to tackle your whole packing process at once, you will be overwhelmed. When you break it down into smaller tasks, especially over time, this gargantuan task becomes quite manageable.

A wonderful gift you can give yourself is time—to give you options, the opportunity to change your mind, and adjust or repack. Packing with a friend's help may make the process more enjoyable.

The God who called you to this move has sent his Holy Spirit to help you in each step, even the practical elements of packing and giving away or selling items. You are not alone.

> *Do not lay up for yourselves treasures on earth, where moth and rust destroy*
> *and where thieves break in and steal, but lay up for yourselves treasures in*
> *heaven, where neither moth nor rust destroys and where thieves do not break*
> *in and steal. For where your treasure is, there your heart will be also.*
> —Matthew 6:19–21

Happiness doesn't have just one address.

—Anonymous

--- **Sample Prayer** ---

Lord, the thought of packing overwhelms me. Please give me discernment for what to take and what to leave, what to sell and what to give away. Allow me to bless others with gifts and trust in your provision for those items I sell—help me to be fair. I want to be generous and prudent; to be a wise steward of what you have given me.

--- **Disclaimer** ---

My views and opinions are my own and may or may not align with any entity with which I am now or have been affiliated. They may also not align with your sending agency, fellowship, or company.

Notes

Notes

CHAPTER THIRTEEN

WRITING NEWSLETTERS

When words are many, transgression is not lacking,
but whoever restrains his lips is prudent.

—Proverbs 10:19

I would have written a shorter letter, but I did not have the time.

—Blaise Pascal

Newsletters are an important connection with your support and prayer network. Your supporters are interested in your life, especially if you live in a culture that differs from theirs, how you are personally, how the Lord is sanctifying you, and how you are shepherding their investment in you. They want to know how to pray for you.

This chapter is broken into three parts: Attributes of an Effective Newsletter, Easy Preparation Steps, and a Sample Framework.

Guiding Principles

- Your newsletter needs to be concise, honest, and regular.
- Be balanced—include some about ministry, some about life, and a fun story.
- Let your pictures tell their thousand words.

──────── ## Attributes of an Effective Newsletter ────────

An easily read, meaningful newsletter is concise, content-rich, and regular.

— *Concise* —

I read and have read many newsletters.

Do not make your reader swim through a sea of words to find the pearls. You need to share how you are, what is happening in your work, how life in your host country differs, and how your reader can help you.

Brevity takes longer to develop, and your communication still needs to be well-written. This section will help you.

Share selectively.
- Your readers do not need to know everything you know.
- **Longer conveys *less* information.**
  - Many people **will not read a long newsletter.**
  - They will miss your points buried in verbose prose.
- For readers who want more,
  - Split your communication.
  - Part One—**the Cliffs Notes** (bullets and short stories)
  - Part Two—**the novel** (longer paragraphs with greater detail)
- Example:
  - Verbose: "R, P, and Q all started reading the Bible with me, but R's next-door neighbor was skeptical and P's mom's hair fell out due to the stress of the police finding out and Q's daughter just had her twenty-first birthday which was a lot of fun."
  - Concise: "Three people in my apartment building started reading the Bible with me. Please pray that God will work through me and give me answers to their questions."
    - Some idea of how you know them will help your reader pray and you to remember what you asked.

Make your points directly.

- **Caveats weaken your statements** and require more words.
- Direct does not mean confrontational or rude.
- Eschew verbosity.

Write in active voice.

- Your newsletter will be **more readable, shorter, and reflect ownership.**
- Write like you would talk to your friend, not like you want to impress your teacher.
- Examples:
  - Passive: "A baptism was held for four people."
    - Active: "We baptized four people."
  - Passive: "It has been communicated that ..."
    - Active: "I read that ..." or "My leader told me that ..."
  - Passive: "The decision was made ..."
    - Active: "I decided ..." or "My leader decided ..."

Use bullets.

- Bullets help your reader **absorb more in less time.**
  - Selectively use **bold fonts** to focus your reader's attention.
- Bullets use fewer words because they may not require full sentences.

Select the correct word.

- **"Words have meanings"** is one of my catchphrases.
  - Incorrect: "I feel like it's rained more this month than usual."
    - Data is not a feeling.
  - Correct: "I think it's rained more this month than usual."
  - Better: Check the facts and be specific.
    - "It rained three inches more this month than usual."
    - "It rained 28 of 30 days versus our normal 10."
- **Vary your word use.**

- ○ Use a good thesaurus (like onelook.com/thesaurus/) to select the correct word.
- ○ Avoid words you do not understand.
- **Avoid fluff, big words, and complex sentences.**
  - ○ Tell **more stories in less space** without losing your reader.
  - ○ Example:
  - ○ Verbose: "I met a beautiful young woman on the college campus one sunny spring day when the flowers were just beginning to bloom. I did not realize then that her faith was in bud as well. Her contemplative worldview conflicted with my Holy Spirit-inspired theological framework and our views on eschatology clearly differed, but we were able to find common ground."
    - ▪ Concise: "I met a woman on our college campus who was interested in hearing the truth from Scripture. We now read the Bible together weekly. Please pray for both of us."
- **Avoid over-spiritualized, trendy language.**
  - ○ This will not resonate with those who are not in your direct circles.
  - ○ Trendy: "I am desirous to …"
    - ▪ Direct: "I want to …"
  - ○ Trendy: "God showed up and …" (Where was our omnipresent God before?)
    - ▪ Direct: "God healed …" or "God spoke …"

Summarize recurring data at the bottom of your newsletter. For example:
- People who agree to read the Bible with me: 1 last month, 50 since arrival
- Faith proclamations: 3 last month, 34 since our arrival
- Churches planted: none last month, 4 since our arrival

Form a small prayer network.
- Share more details more frequently with a few people via secure communications.
- This reduces the perceived need to share more with your entire distribution list.

— *Content-Rich* —

Your organization may need detailed monthly statistics, but most of your readers do not. They want short stories and concise updates with photos.

Include these topics for content-rich communication.

Share how God is working.
- How has he changed you?
- How has he changed the lives of those with whom you interact?

Be honest.
- **If life is hard,** briefly describe why and ask for prayers.
- Do not inflate your results.
  - **Dry periods** are normal in all ministry.
  - Share them and ask for prayers.
- **Be balanced**—share what you love or blessings you experience or witness.
- **Be honest.**

Share a short anecdote.
- No more than two.
- Example: "We prayed as we drove to lunch that the Lord would open a door. About fifteen minutes in, our hostess started asking us spiritual questions, and the Holy Spirit directed our answers. (I know it was him because I am not that smart!)"

Show, don't tell.
- Keep your "shows" brief, but colorful.
- Tell: "I'm really busy."
  - Show: "This past month I've done x, y, and z."
- Tell: "Living here is hard."
  - Show: "People ignore my friendly greetings. I cannot order a meal without help. Buying groceries takes all afternoon."

Share prayer requests and answered prayers.
- **Start with answered prayers.**
  - Even when the answer is "no."
- **Ask people to do something—pray!**
  - Keep to **four or five** prayer points.
- **Summarize** rather than listing everyone and every need.
  - "Please pray for the <number> people who will read the Bible with me this month."
  - "Three people want to be baptized. Please pray they will follow through."
- If you need financial support, ask for prayer first.
  - Praying people are open to God's direction.
- Ask how you can **pray for those praying for you!**
  - **Pray as soon as you read** requests and **respond immediately.**

People love pictures.
- **"A picture is worth a thousand words"** (Fred R. Barnard or Arthur Brisbane).
  - Therefore, your caption requires only a few.
  - Make your caption informational for those who only look at pictures.
  - Do your photos tell a story, progress chronologically, or reflect the flow of your newsletter?
- Your readers want to **see how your life "there" differs** from their lives "here".
  - Show the store where you buy your food or favorite lunch place.
  - What do street signs look like?
  - Can you capture traffic?
- **Limit family photos** to no more than three.
- Share **short videos.**
  - One- to two-minute videos can pack a big story in a small package.
  - Make the link name compelling.
  - **Use selectively**—major changes, new baby, national events, etc.
  - Some of your recipients cannot download or will not follow links.
  - Share a summary for those who cannot or will not watch.

- ○ Moveyoumedia.com or a similar site will help you make effective videos.
- Remember to **obscure faces and names** and **be careful with backgrounds** if you are in a sensitive environment.

Share upcoming changes or the potential for them.
- **Do not surprise your supporters** by communicating major changes after the fact.
- Invite them to **pray with you as you evaluate** your future.
- Might you lose a few because of your uncertainty?
    - ○ Maybe—God will provide if he has called you to change.
- **A short bullet** in your newsletter with an off-cycle **"special edition"** to provide the details, or addendum at the bottom, is one way to address this.
    - ○ Keep this additional content brief and content-rich.

Humor helps.
- You do not lose any holy points by infusing a bit of humor.
- Use it judiciously—you are not writing a comic book.

Additional ideas
- Share **national or cultural events** (e.g., royal wedding) in pictures with a short description.
- Some people like to share what they are reading to create a connection with their readers.

— Regular —

If you send your updates out on a regular schedule, you not only accumulate less to share (shorter), but it helps people know when to look for your next update.

- **Monthly** works well.
    - ○ Not less than quarterly.

- If **you are too busy** to communicate regularly, evaluate your calendar.
  - Irregularity reflects a **lack of discipline or priority.**
- **Weekly is too frequent.**
  - Several notes a week become spam—readers will tune you out.
  - You are not the center of your reader's world.
- **Do not apologize** for a delayed newsletter, but do not make it a habit.
  - **Share specific reasons** for the delay.
  - "I've been busy" just says your reader is unimportant.

Easy Preparation Steps

A little initial time investment with minimal ongoing commitment will yield pain-free newsletter writing.

1. **Create a framework** that you can reuse each month.
   - Make a copy of the last month's, rename it, and replace the information.
   - A regular format helps your reader know where to find what is of most interest to them.
   - See example in the "Sample Framework" section.
2. **Make notes** as you observe or experience "newsletter-worthy" events.
   - Store them in a folder on your phone or in an on-line document for ready retrieval.
3. **File photos** as soon as you take them.
   - Keep them **smaller than a few 100k kilobytes** (kb) to avoid spam filters.
     - You can find free compression tools online.
     - We **email the picture** from our iPhone to our Gmail, which gives us the option to select the size.
       - We have had no problems with "medium" and ten or fewer photos.
   - Save your photo with the **format yy.mm <description>** where yy.mm is the month you plan to use the photo.

- E.g., Family photo for the September 2024 newsletter: 24.09 Family
- When you prepare your newsletter, open the folder and sort descending by name.
- This process saves you time, prevents the distraction of searching for photos, and helps you remember what you planned to share.

Sample Framework

This is the order we have found successful for our newsletters. Depending on your delivery service, you may need to make adjustments. Ensure your reader can **easily identify** what content is current.

Adjust the order if you have an important or urgent prayer request or photo to share.

Subject Line

- **Capture your reader's attention.**
  - "I thought we would die."
  - "A month we will never forget"
  - "Surprised by blessings"
  - "Our work may change"
- As "unholy" as it sounds, **you are competing for your reader's time.**

Title
- **Sets the theme** for the newsletter.
- Should be the same as the subject line in your email.

Opening
- This is the introduction to your newsletter and **needs to reflect the title.**
- **Glorify God.**

- A **concise, well-written paragraph or two** that expands your theme.
- From the subject lines above, answer:
    - What caused you to think you would die? What was the outcome?
    - Why will you never forget this month?
    - What blessings did you receive and why were you surprised?
    - Why will your work change? How?

Updates

- Use **bullet points.**
- Share your experiences, what you are reading, things that have positively or negatively impacted you, a day in your life, etc.
- These may or may not reflect your opening.

Prayers (call to action)

- Use bullet points.
- Answered prayers and requests.
    - Limit to four to six of each.
- Ask your readers to share their prayer requests with you.

Pictures

- Place them **towards the end.**
    - Give your "photos only" readers a chance to see bullets as they scroll past.
- Use **short captions** to tell a story.
- A great place to **introduce a little humor.**

Recurring data

- This is a good spot for updating your table with recurring data.
- A table can be a good way to present this information.

Contact information / prior newsletters

- Link to your contribution site if you expressed financial need.

- A link to prior newsletters is important for new subscribers.

Before you Send your Newsletter

Use a **grammar-checking tool**, even if you are a natural writer.

- Online tools are available for free.

Write it. Read it. Time it.
- If it takes more than a few minutes to read, shorten it.
- When you review it, ask: "**How can I use fewer words?**"
  - Use a thesaurus (like onelook.com/thesaurus/).

Write, set aside, share with a pre-reader, update, then send.
- **Ensure readability and picture sizing** for phone and computer.
- You are not vying for a Pulitzer Prize so **do not agonize over your writing**.
  - Your readers will forgive you a few errors, especially in exchange for brevity and active voice.

Encouragement

Writing newsletters can be intimidating. They do not need to be. Pray for discernment regarding what and how to share. Build a framework once and reuse it. Make notes and save photos as you go along.

Your readers want to know how you are, to gain some insights into your world, and to learn about the work you do. They do not require perfect prose, and brevity will overcome a multitude of errors. Write to inform, not to impress. Your goal is to glorify God in your work, not to point to a perfect life.

If any of you lacks wisdom, let him ask God, who gives generously
to all without reproach, and it will be given him.

—James 1:5

The scariest moment is always just before you start.

—Stephen King

Sample Prayer

Lord, I do not like writing newsletters. Help me to honor you by communicating succinctly, honestly, and regularly with those who support me. Please free my mind to write and provide me with the discipline to record and plan.

I pray that each newsletter I send will turn people to you even as I share humorous anecdotes along with stories and pictures of my life and the culture here.

Disclaimer

*My views and opinions are my own and may or may not align with
any entity with which I am now or have been affiliated. They may also
not align with your sending agency, fellowship, or company.*

Additional Resources

Weyeneth, Sandy, *Writing Exceptional Missionary Newsletters*
Young, Amy, *Enjoying Newsletters*

Notes

Notes

CHAPTER FOURTEEN

SENDING

Now to him who is able to do far more abundantly than all that we
ask or think, according to the power at work within us …
—Ephesians 3:20

You are not raising support, but supporters. Technically, we are
'supporter raising.' We are raising people, not money.
—Steve Shadrach,
The God Ask

If you are a "goer," you typically have "senders," which may be organizations, a sending fellowship, a company, individual supporters, or some combination thereof. This chapter is for them.

— Guiding Principles —

- Ensure a specific church leader will regularly contact your cross-cultural worker.
- The worker your send is like the church's child—care for them as your own. Increase your knowledge and understanding of your worker's new ecosystem—sending agency, receiving team, work city, etc.).
- Ensure expectations are clear—what the church will do or provide and what you expect your worker to do, how and how often.

—————————— **Senders** ——————————

The way you support can reduce or increase anxiety. These suggestions are to foster the former.

Connect with your goer.
- **Pray for them** and tell them when you do—this is a great encouragement to one far from home.
  - Pray for them communally as well (keeping in mind security restrictions) and tell them when you have.
- **Reach out**—send an email, voice mail, or video message.
  - Put this on your calendar to do once a quarter or so.
    - The longer a worker is on the field, the fewer contacts they receive.
  - A physical card is a thoughtful gift.
    - Send with someone who will visit if there is no effective mail service.
- Especially if you are part of their care team, **follow up as committed.**

Help them when they visit or return.
- Read the "Visiting" and "Returning" chapters for practical ways to help.
- Your goer needs people who will **ask and listen.**
  - Train others to do the same.
  - Give your goer(s) time to answer you thoroughly and give them your **undivided attention.**
  - Allow for some silence and push a bit if you get a short answer.
- **Examples of good questions:**
  - What has been the most rewarding?
  - What has been the most frustrating?
  - How has your physical health been? Your mental health?
  - Is there something we can do to support you better or differently?
  - What blessings did God give you that surprised you?

- How did God use you in ways you did not expect?
- Were you able to form any relationships with locals?
- How did your local relationships turn out?
  - Note: If badly, offer more listening time.
- What losses did you experience?
  - Have you been able to grieve them?
  - How can I help you?
- What would you like to share that I did not ask?
  - With this last one in particular, provide ample time to answer, even if it includes awkward silence.
- For those on home leave who will return to the field:
  - How can I support you when you return?

Financial supporters
- Ensure your **payments arrive on time.**
- Provide as much advanced notice as possible if you need to reduce or discontinue your contributions.

Sending Fellowship Representatives

Here are additional suggestions if you represent the sending fellowship and/or organization.

Plan at least one visit
- This should be **someone in leadership** or who can otherwise represent your church, especially during a worker's first term.
- Discuss the following details to find the best time to go.
  - Team travel windows
  - Local holidays that will disrupt or enhance your visit
  - What they would like or need you to bring them
    - Share any size, volume, or weight restrictions.

- Gather cards from friends and family. This is a wonderful surprise.

Review their care plan and ensure you are part of it.
- **Provide the care you commit.**
- Read the "Self-Care" chapter for additional insights.

Missions pastors, **share the load!**
- **The church sent** this person, couple, or family.
- **The church needs to meet their needs.**
  - Do not shoulder the load alone.
- Ensure someone representing the church also asks the questions above.
  - This is not an interview, but important care from their sending fellowship.

Encouragement

Your part of the great commission is important—there are not goers without senders.

Expect to miss the person you put on a plane, whom you may not see again for months or years. Place a reminder somewhere in your house or office to pray for them. Send them emails or messages of encouragement (complying with any security restrictions they give you).

If you support them financially, set this up to be done automatically or set reminders in your calendar. Ask the Lord to show you how to pray for them and when. Let your goer know when you have prayed for them, as it encourages them.

> *For God is not unjust so as to overlook your work and the love that you have shown for his name in serving the saints, as you still do.*
> —Hebrews 6:10

> *The best remedy for a sick church is to put it on a missionary diet.*
> —David Livingstone

Sample Prayer

Lord, help me to provide for those I support financially and in prayer, in their absence and when they return. Help me to listen for needs they do not express, to recognize pain that is not spoken, and to point them to you when discouraged, lonely, or sad.

Disclaimer

My views and opinions are my own and may or may not align with any entity with which I am now or have been affiliated. They may also not align with your sending agency, fellowship, or company.

Additional Resources

Bell, Bradley, Mike Easton, et al., *The Sending Church Applied*

Bradley, Zach, et al., *Receiving Sent Ones During Reentry*

Shadrach, Steve and Scott Morton, *The God Ask*

Notes

Notes

CHAPTER FIFTEEN

LEADING

Where there is no guidance, a people falls, but in an abundance of counselors there is safety.
—Proverbs 11:14

When you delegate tasks, you create followers. When
you delegate authority, you create leaders.

—Craig Groeschel,
founder of Life Church

This chapter is for you, team leader, even if you are in the role reluctantly.

Some expect the team leader to be the primary teacher, best speaker of your host language, and most experienced in your team's mission (planting, discipling, sharing, etc.). These are **unreasonable and unhealthy expectations.** Your highest work priority must be leading.

Guiding Principles

- Leadership must be your first priority after God and family, not language or your other work. Leading is your primary ministry.
- You need a plan to lead, develop, and care for those on your team. (Note that this does not mean you need to be the primary trainer or caregiver, but you have a plan for these to be met.)
- Know what you do well and either eliminate or delegate what you do not.

What Leaders Need to Do

Set **reasonable expectations** for yourself and your team.
- Unreasonable expectations lead to **burnout.**
- Prevent **scope creep.**
  - As team members come and go, do not simply redistribute their workload.
  - Work with your team to see what work can be eliminated, deferred, or transferred to a local partner (who also needs to have their expectations adjusted).

Cast vision.
- Your team members need **direction** and counsel.
- If you did not create your team's vision, unless it is broken, keep casting it!

Maintain perspective.
- "We are not building God's kingdom. He is building his kingdom, and we are praying for the privilege of being involved." (Francis Schaeffer)
- God has given you the privilege to lead his people to do his work.
  - **Your identity must be a child of God, not a leader.**
  - Leading is simply what you do.

Follow your MOU.
- If your team does not have an MOU, create one.
- See the Contracting chapter for more information.
- **Discuss it with your team** and ensure it is reasonable.
- The MOU needs to be two-way.
  - It should include what you expect from those you lead and what they can expect from you.

Make decisions in a timely manner.
- "In any moment of decision, the best thing you can do is the right thing, the next best thing is the wrong thing, and the worst thing you can do is nothing." (Author unknown, but attributed to Theodore Roosevelt)
- Delay creates anxiety for your team.
- **Avoid the ready-aim-aim-aim syndrome.**
  - You will make mistakes—that is part of decision-making.
  - Learn from them, adjust quickly, apologize if necessary, then move on.
  - See John Wayne's quote at the end of this chapter.

Be Responsive.
- Respond to messages within a few hours, and emails within twenty-four hours, especially from your team.
  - **A short reply** with a date for an answer is better than no answer.
- If you promise something for a future date, make sure to follow through.
  - Do not string this out.

Delegate.
- Model how to ask for help.
- **Empower team members.**

- ○ "Assume God is speaking to and leading others on your team. Include them in your decision-making process as much as practical." (Serge Leadership Lab[8], Module 2, Part 2)
- Find those on your team who **do things better than you do.**
- When you delegate, adjust other work or study expectations for the person to whom you delegate.
  - ○ **Do not simply increase workload.**
- Some areas to **delegate:**
  - ○ **Care**—You still have the final responsibility, but you can discuss a structure for someone else to manage and follow up.
  - ○ **Administrative and scheduling tasks**—Would hiring a remote administrative person help if there is not someone on your team who would enjoy such work?
  - ○ **Event planning**—Team members often enjoy this kind of work.
  - ○ **Teaching**—Find others in your network who can teach what you do not know. Focus on teaching your areas of strength.

Minimize required permissions.
- Empower team members to make most decisions in their personal lives.
- Notification makes sense for planning and security reasons, but minimize the permissions required for team members to live their lives, enjoy their vacations, take required visa runs, date, have children, etc.
  - ○ One idea is a vacation window when permission is not needed (just notification), with permission required only outside that time frame.
  - ○ Notifications should be made well ahead of the absence.

See the "Sample MOU" at www.DHarakalAuthor.org for examples.

---

[8] serge.org/leadership-lab/

Plan ahead.
- **Schedule events** at least three months in advance.
- **Recurring team events** need to be regular (same day and time) so people can plan their weeks.
- If scheduling is not something you do well, delegate it to a team member who excels in logistics.
- If no one does, rotate the duty among team members and leaders.

Meet regularly with other leaders.
- This helps protect you from myopic thinking and navigate new challenges.
  - Find leaders from other organizations and agencies.
- Some challenges that you can expect to face, and need to work through with other leaders:
  - How to contextualize your ministry while protecting Scripture's truths
  - Navigate political issues that could affect you or your team
  - Work through theological differences in your team or partner teams
  - Make time for your health to model good time management
  - Adapt to your team's needs as they change, or with different individuals

Find a **leadership accountability partner.**
- **Befriend other leaders** in your context.
- **Meet regularly.**
  - No less frequent than monthly, though more frequent is better.
  - An in-person group is ideal.
  - **Discuss challenges and ideas; share successes and failures.**
- You should have a **supervisor** or someone with oversight.

Be approachable.
- **Listen to those you lead.**
- Invite feedback, especially from reserved team members.

- Become comfortable with silence—some people need time to formulate their thoughts.

Filter potential team members.
- Does the sending church fully endorse them and take responsibility for them?
    - If not, do not invite them to join your team.
- Did they recently change churches?
    - This may indicate that their prior fellowship did not support their plans.
- Get a **list of medications** they take (if possible, based on privacy laws).
    - Are they available in your host country or nearby?
    - A candidate dependent on mental health drugs may require a level of care your team may not be able to provide, especially if needs change or medications become unavailable.
    - This is not just theory—learn from others' experiences.
- These are not theoretical scenarios.
    - **Learn from others' mistakes!**

Read Chapter 2 in *Bully Pulpit* and make sure you do not slide into any abusive habits.

——— What Leaders Need to Avoid ———

Be cautious of **close friendships** with those you lead.
- Close friendship with team members you lead can create a conflict of interest and become a form of nepotism.
    - This is most true when the team is young and inexperienced and the leader is older with more experience.
    - An exception is a team of equals or peers.
- One of you may need to change teams if you tend towards favoritism or lose objectivity.

Do not **burn out team members.**

- Recognize **different capacities.**
  - ○ Expecting one-size-fits-all is a clear sign of a poor leader
- Ensure they take time off by modeling **sabbaths and vacations.**
- Know the signs of burnout—for their sake and yours.

Do not schedule events or retreats **hastily or over weekends** or holidays.
- Even if it is a retreat, if it is required, it needs to be part of the work week.
  - ○ **Scheduling weekend events is disrespectful** of your team's personal time, even if it is common for others serving on the field.
  - ○ Your team needs their sabbath and rest.
  - ○ If the weekend is the only option, provide time off the week before or after and encourage those in full-time language to cancel those days.
- Schedule at least a month in advance.
  - ○ Three months in advance is better, even if you do not have all the details.
  - ○ Give people time to adjust their plans.

Do not call last-minute required meetings or events.
- These frustrate team members and add to their stress.
- Save those for true emergencies.
- **Announcements are rarely emergencies**—plan ahead.

Do not present your team as a family.
- Scripture does describe those who leave to do the work of the Gospel in terms of family, and it is a worthy goal, but do not make promises you and your team cannot keep.
- The expectation **implies relationships or obligations** that may not be realistic.
- This too often **leads to unmet expectations,** especially for singles or those with unhealthy families of origin.

Let go of full-time seminary or other full-time commitments while you lead.

- Coaching or short-term training courses will help you hone your skills.
- Avoid anything that regularly competes with your leadership (during working hours).

For Reluctant Leaders

Thank you, reluctant leaders! You stepped in to lead because no one else would, outside your comfort zone, without training, and have inherited a team you did not recruit or build. You may also operate under an MOU you did not write and do not like.

Your task is challenging, and **you are not alone.**

I want to help you flourish in this role until you are replaced or your team disbands.

Embrace what you can from the section above, but most importantly:

Adjust your expectations.
- Leadership is **time consuming**.
- You are the shepherd for your flock, and sometimes **sheep bite.**
  - If you were previously a team member, the change in roles will be awkward as relationships change.
- If you are in full-time language, **take a break.**
- If you are in seminary or other school, **take a break.**

Delegate!
- Untrained leaders tend to hold on to too much.
- Ask other leaders what tasks you should delegate, permissions you can relinquish, or roles you can share.
- Delegate to **avoid burnout** and **empower your team.**

Own your team's MOU.
- If needed, adapt it to fit your team with their input.
  - Make it functional, not perfect, for expediency.

Promote the team's vision.
- This provides needed consistency.
- Reluctant leaders I have known (and there are many) are not visionaries.
  - This is not a character flaw—different people have different gifts.
- Only change the vision if you plan to lead long-term, as frequent vision changes create disruption.
- If you inherit a team that no longer adheres to the vision, unless they have a common new vision, disband the team and encourage participants to pursue teams whose vision aligns with theirs.

Do what you need to do.
- **Get a mentor** and ask many questions.
- **Sabbath and rest!**
- **Set direction** and **manage the work** (not the people).
- **Develop team members**
  - Either directly or through courses or other mentors, help those you lead mature in their theology and skills.
- **Care**
  - Create time to listen—get to know those you lead.
  - Help your team build their self-care network (see the Self-Care chapter).
    - You can delegate the management and tracking of self-care.

Do not do what does not need to be done!
- Do not enroll for a long, involved leadership class unless you plan to lead going forward.
  - You will end up overwhelmed.
  - A mentor will serve you better than a long course if you only plan to serve short term.
- Do not expect to be everything to your team.
- Delegate or eliminate those functions you cannot fulfill.
  - Know yourself, your skills, and your limitations.

- An online, low-impact course might be refreshing and helpful without being overwhelming.
  - The Leadership Lab from grace.northpass.com is a good option.

Encouragement

A leader's most important work, the work you are called to do, is leading. Others can teach, or model how to open a conversation, how to plant a church, or help with language. Delegate to those you lead to lighten your load and empower them. Cast and recast vision.

I use the term **reluctant leader** for those who did not plan to lead, but I do not mean to imply that God did not plan for you to lead, at least for now. Lacking the desire to lead is not a character flaw. God designed some to lead and some to follow—there would be no team without followers!

> *Do nothing from selfish ambition or conceit, but in humility count others more significant than yourselves. Let each of you look not only to his own interests, but also to the interests of others.*
>
> —Philippians 2:3–4

> *What's the secret of success? Right decisions.*
> *How do you make right decisions? Experience.*
> *How do you get experience? Wrong decisions.*
>
> —John Wayne

Sample Prayer

Lord, help me shepherd as you shepherded. Show me how to protect and empower my team to reach their full potential in the work they do for you, to focus on you first and then your work. Please provide me with other leaders as co-laborers and mentors.

I want your heart for those I lead, even when my sheep bite. I need your patience, wisdom, and vision. Holy Spirit, please lead through me.

─── **Disclaimer** ───

My views and opinions are my own and may or may not align with any entity with which I am now or have been affiliated. They may also not align with your sending agency, fellowship, or company.

─── **Additional Resources** ───

Grace Academy Leadership Lab www.grace.northpass.com

Taylor, Dr. and Mrs. Howard, *Hudson Taylor's Spiritual Secret*

Notes

--------------------------- **Notes** ---------------------------

CHAPTER SIXTEEN

SINGLENESS

I praise you, for I am fearfully and wonderfully made. Wonderful
are your works; my soul knows it very well.

—Psalm 139:14

We need to remind ourselves, daily, that our singleness is not for us but for the Lord.

—Sam Allberry

Back in the dark ages, before social media existed (so there is no evidence), I was single during college—and my memory has not completely failed. I have mentored many single people and my wife and I raised two into adulthood, so I do have some insight into the joys and struggles of singleness. Several single friends on the field shared their insights for this chapter. Sam Allberry's book, *7 Myths About Singleness*, helped me understand current challenges and opportunities.

Some of you choose to remain single for the sake of the Gospel (Matthew 19:12). Some of you would like to be married but have not found the right partner. For those in the latter group, you may hope that the right person is right around the corner, or have resigned yourself to a life of singleness against your wishes. I pray you will be completely content with Jesus alone in any of these scenarios. Though I am married with children and grandchildren, I pray this for myself as well.

Guiding Principles

- God must be sufficient for you.
- Know what is culturally appropriate and safe.
- Invest in local friends outside your team, especially those from your primary culture or a proximate culture first, then locals.
- Women—be extremely wary of local men's advances.

Field Realities

Loneliness is prevalent.

- Though not unique to singles, it is more pronounced.
- **Build your community**—no one will build it for you.
  - Invite others to participate in a hobby you love or develop a new one.
  - Make new friends, including locals.
  - Same-gender single friends are especially important if most on your team are married.

Do not expect your team to feel like family.

- Many team leaders call their team "family."
- This may be **a painful disconnect** when it does not feel like one to you.
- Your team may change over time.
  - A sense of family develops organically, not by declaration.

You have **greater flexibility** than your married peers.

- You can focus more on the Lord's service, as Paul notes in 1 Corinthians 7:32-35.
- **This can be frustrating**.
  - More of your team's burden may fall on you because leaders or others believe you have more capacity or free time.

- o **Know your limits and set boundaries.**
  - ▪ You need rest and refreshment and breaks as much as anyone.
  - ▪ Say "yes" when you can, but say "no" when you need to.
- o Single females are often "assumed" babysitters.
  - ▪ If this is not why you joined the team, set boundaries/limits.
  - ▪ If this is not an area where you flourish, be honest with those who ask you. (I had to do this myself!)
- o Discuss with your team before this leads to bitterness.

Host-country roommates

- Local roommates can be a way to enhance your language and cultural understanding.
  - o **They can also be a disaster,** which results in a disruption to your ministry and may result in expulsion from your host country.
- They must be mentally stable.
  - o As appealing as the desire to "rescue" someone from an abusive or dangerous environment, unless you are trained in such, they are more likely to take you down with them.
- Ensure your roommate(s) have **experience living on their own.**
- They need a **sustained source of income** unless you plan to support them financially.
  - o Income must be sustained, which can be evidenced by the prior bullet unless the other roommates were paying for them.
  - o Income is not sustained if preceded by "I'm looking," or "I might have something with my cousin," etc.
  - o **Beware** of becoming the unplanned surrogate parents of an irresponsible and potentially dangerous adult child.
- You may choose to house someone **temporarily in an emergency,** but you need to set out from the beginning how long and hold to that.

Sexual temptation may be elevated.

- **Sin tendencies generally increase** for everyone on the field due to loneliness, lack of safeguards, and the enemy's deliberate focus—he hates cross-cultural ministry!
- **Do not struggle alone.**
  - The books by Deepak Reju in the "Reading" appendix can help.
  - This is not unique to you, but rampant in the mission field.

For Single Women

I thank my single female colleagues for their input on this section.

If you serve in a more conservative, patriarchal, honor-shame culture, your life will present more challenges than your male counterparts experience.

Anecdote: We are from Texas, where every stranger is a potential friend and the common courtesy is to make eye contact and say "hello" or "howdy." Moving to a country where unmarried men and women are forbidden to interact came as a particular shock to my outgoing, friendly wife, and added another layer to her transition challenge.

Ladies, prepare yourselves for the following possibilities—or probabilities:

- Teenage and other young women: pre-teen boys and young **unmarried men may constantly harass you.**
  - In some cultures, the taunts may be "harmless," but are nonetheless unwanted, tiresome, and humiliating.
  - In others, this may become dangerous.
  - Know the difference!
- Women may experience **greater social judgment** and attract unkind looks from other women who seem to pride themselves in their "modesty," particularly in a Muslim culture where some (or most) women cover their entire body.
  - Some even cover their eyes!
- **Do not exacerbate the situation.**
  - Ensure your **dress is modest.**

- o Foreigners are often given more leeway, but do not push it.

Beware of relationships with host-country men.
- As much as locals may express their dislike of your passport country (especially the U.S.A.), most want a visa.
- Beware of men who seem eligible and want to develop a relationship.
  - o Even men who claim to be Christians.
    - ▪ Look for the fruits of the spirit and evidence of their faith.
  - o Sadly, in most cases, this is **about the visa, not about you**.
    - ▪ Time will bear out most false pursuits.
  - o A local man rushing you into a relationship is even more of a red flag in a cross-cultural context than in your passport country.
- **Invite others** on your team, team leaders, and family to discuss any relationship with a local man early so that they can protect your heart from pursuing a union that may not be what it seems.
  - o There are godly, wonderful local men, but you must be more cautious.
  - o If you date local men, understand what dating means in your culture, what is acceptable, and what is not.
- **Guard yourself physically.**
  - o Unplanned pregnancy can be a means to force a marriage—or become deadly.

You need safe men.
- **In paternalistic and religiously conservative host countries,** an unmarried woman in her twenties or thirties is an anomaly.
- Married couples who can present you as a daughter or sister provide excellent protection, especially if you need to visit a police station for a visa or renewal.
- Single men on your team who can present you as a sister can provide you protection against unwanted advances in social settings, restaurants, etc.
- This may require great humility, especially if you came from a country where being a single woman represented social achievement or elevated status.

You need close female friends.

- When someone harasses you or you are frustrated by restrictions society places on you, you need a friend to **discuss your experiences.**
  - Someone "readily available" is ideal.
- There are more single women than single men on the field, unfortunately.
  - You are not alone, and it is not your fault.
  - Many other women share your experience.
  - **Reach out to them!**

Encouragement

God knows your heart. He knows your desires and temptations, and knows what works for you, uniquely for you, not "even though" you are single but "because" you are single.

Serve God in the way only you can and glorify him through your unique experience, wisdom, and perspective.

> *Only let each person lead the life that the Lord has assigned to him, and to which God has called him. This is my rule in all the churches.*
> —1 Corinthians 7:17

> *If God is going to write your love story, he's going to first need your pen.*
> —Eric Ludy

Sample Prayer

Lord, be sufficient for me. Unless or until you bring me a spouse, help me to run to you first when I am lonely.

Jesus, as long as you call me to singleness, let my life reflect the complete life you lived in the companionship of the Father and Holy Spirit.

———— Disclaimer ————

My views and opinions are my own and may or may not align with any entity with which I am now or have been affiliated. They may also not align with your sending agency, fellowship, or company.

———— Additional Resources ————

Allberry, Sam, *7 Myths About Singleness*

Reju, Deepak, *Pornography: Fighting for Purity (31-Day Devotionals for Life)*

Reju, Deepak and Jonathan Holmes, *Rescue Plan*

Reju, Deepak and Jonathan Holmes, *Rescue Skills*

Notes

Notes

CHAPTER SEVENTEEN

MARRIAGE

Above all, keep loving one another earnestly, since love covers a multitude of sins.

—1 Peter 4:8

*A good marriage isn't something you find; it's something
you make and you have to keep on making it.*

—Gary Thomas

The enemy hates marriage. He also hates evangelism. Put those two together and it is no surprise that married couples in missions are particular targets for him. If he can disrupt your marriage, he receives a double benefit because it also undermines your ministry and may remove you from the field.

The needs of a marriage on the field are not fundamentally different from the needs of a marriage in any other context, and most pressures on the field are not so different from those elsewhere, but there are some elements that contribute uniquely to marital discord.

Guiding Principles

- A marriage is not flourishing unless each spouse is.
- Give your spouse extra grace—seek to love him or her as God does.
- You must agree on your long-term goals regarding mission and location—let God arbitrate if not.
- Your marriage must reflect the Gospel to others.

Cross-Cultural Marriage Challenges

Calling differences may lead to conflict.

- **Your partner may blame you** for their discomfort and dissatisfaction, even if you both felt called to your new home.
  - **Do not allow resentment** to fester, either of you!
- The degree to which **you miss family** may be different.
  - **Physical distance is compounded by time zone differences.**
  - Family and friend **connections must be balanced** with meeting each other's needs.
- **Language learning** may become a point of tension.
  - It is **exhausting and frustrating**.
  - If one catches on quicker than the other, remember that "do not compare" applies to your spouse as well.
  - **Provide extra grace and encouragement.**

Locals may treat husbands and wives differently.

- When different social rules and expectations apply to men and women, one spouse may feel more separated than the other.
- One may have more freedom than the other.
  - E.g., men in conservative Muslim countries have many fewer social restrictions.

- Anecdote: We are from Texas, where every stranger is a potential friend and the common courtesy is to make eye contact and say "hello" or "howdy." Moving to a country where unmarried men and women are forbidden to interact came as a particular shock to my outgoing, friendly wife, when shopkeepers and men in general ignored her. This added another layer to her transition challenge. (Copied from the "Singleness" chapter.)

Covering may have physical effects, especially for women.
- In a culture where clothing must go from neck to wrist to ankle, Vitamin D deficiency may lead to a depressed mood if you moved from a sun-loving climate.
- Talk to your doctor.
- Add more lighting in your home, especially "full spectrum" lighting.

You may suffer from **over-togetherness**.
- Yes, I made up that diagnosis.
- This may be the first time you have been together all day, every day.
- You may experience a **loss of independence.**
- **Seek balance**—it is not wrong to benefit from some independent time.

—— Benefits of Marriage for Cross-Cultural Life ——

You have a **built-in sounding board.**
- **You have a partner you know,** rather than a roommate you have to figure out
- You have a **shared history.**
- You understand each other's breaking points.
- Proximity offers you a chance to catch trends early.

Cross-cultural living refines your marriage.
- You have different opportunities to grow closer to your spouse and your Lord.
- Let iron sharpen iron.

Some cultures revere marriage, which will help you integrate and help your ministry.

———— Advice for all Married Couples ————

The work the Lord called you to do may be only part of his purpose. A greater goal may be to refine you and strengthen your marriage.

Meet with God.
- **Ask him to show you** the person he sees in your spouse.
- **Pray together.**
  - Do not allow "busyness" to interfere.
    - **Your spouse needs you.**
    - God can accomplish his goals without you.
  - **Do not give the enemy a foothold.**
- **Confess, repent, sacrifice, repeat.**
  - We are all called to serve our Lord, in part, by serving others.
  - Start with your spouse.

Set appropriate expectations.
- **Target a 100/0 marriage.**
  - A 50/50 marriage is not possible, and that goal leads to frustration.
- Do not attempt equal effort.
  - If you are willing to do 100% and expect nothing, you will appreciate your spouse for anything they do and be increasingly sanctified.

Invest in your marriage.
- You need regular "**date nights**," at least monthly.
- Husbands, this is your job.
  - **Do not stop courting your wife.**
- **Parents, get away without the children** for a weekend a few times a year.
  - This helps you and your children.

Meet with others.

- Meet regularly with **marriage mentors.**
  - They should be of you.
  - Ideally, they knew you as a couple before you left.
  - If you can meet in person, that is a bonus.
  - **Give them permission to confront and correct you.**
- **Invite singles** on your team for a meal. at least one life phase ahead
  - They need your community and can feel overlooked.
  - Giving to others returns more than the investment.
- **Attend a theologically sound local church** in a language you speak and understand well, if possible.
  - **You need community.**
  - **Scripture commands it** in Hebrews 10:24–25, et al.
  - You **need support** and accountability.
  - Your next best option is a house church.
  - If you can, avoid just "doing church with the two of us."

Encouragement

Marriage in cross-cultural ministry has unique challenges. Two sinners living together in the pressure cooker of cultural confusion and language fog will result in a beautiful picture of Christ and his church or boil over in a mess.

Give more grace than you expect in return, and pray for the Lord to show you the person he knows, sees, hears, and understands in your spouse. He will.

If "all God does" during your time in cross-cultural ministry is refine your marriage, your time in the field will be a resounding success. Of course, if he does that in your marriage, he will use you not only for what you think he sent you to do, but in many other ways you may never realize.

So they are no longer two but one flesh. What therefore
God has joined together, let not man separate.

—Mark 10:8b-9

A happy marriage is the union of two good forgivers.

—Ruth Bell Graham

Sample Prayer

Lord, help me see my spouse the way you see him or her, to love them the way you love them, to become the husband or wife that you want me to be for them. Please use this time in our marriage to grow closer to you and to each other.

Please show us those to whom we need to extend hospitality. Help us to provide the family setting that singles on our team or in our community need.

Disclaimer

My views and opinions are my own and may or may not align with any entity with which I am now or have been affiliated. They may also not align with your sending agency, fellowship, or company.

Additional Resources

Eggerichs, Dr. Emerson, *Love and Respect*

Henderson, John, *Catching Foxes*

Re|engage—reengage.org

A Weekend to Remember (for those who visit the U.S.)—
familylife.com/weekend-to-remember/

Notes

Notes

CHAPTER EIGHTEEN

PARENTING

Train up a child in the way he should go, and when he is old, he will not depart from it.
—Proverbs 22:6 (KJV)

If I could have done anything differently, I would have prioritized our children's needs.
—Cross-cultural Worker,
retiring after forty years

*Children are not a distraction from more important
work. They are the most important work.*

—C. S. Lewis

God loans us his children to parent for him. I hope that intimidates you as it did me!

I love children, which is not something I would have said before having our own. The Lord blessed us with two and, as of this writing, he has further blessed us with two grandchildren and one on the way.

Parenting is a challenge—anywhere. We developed and taught parenting courses for over twenty-five years, not because we were perfect parents, but because we needed to keep learning!

Section one addresses topics or challenges specific to raising children in a third-culture context. Section two addresses some of the positive parenting and prevalent parenting mistakes I see regularly—on or off the field.

Thank you to the parents with young children who have provided me with input for this chapter.

Guiding Principles

- If a child is not flourishing, the family is not flourishing.
- You are shepherding God's children for him—model the Gospel.
- Behavior must be based on Biblical principles, not societal norms.
- Your relationship with your child should be high warmth/high discipline.
- You should enjoy time with your children, as should other adults and children.
- Plan for each school year in advance, and look into different options for different children based on their changing needs.

What Kind of Parent Are You?

Some of you enjoy well-adjusted children whom you taught to navigate the challenges of cross-cultural living, the result of tireless, thoughtful, focused effort.

Others of you are new to the field or considering moving, and wonder how you will navigate this new season with children and what unique challenges lay ahead.

Still others may have raised your children on the field with no one to support you. Or, worse, the functional model you learned from others resulted in children who are disrespectful, disobedient, and unruly, leaving them discontented and confused, and this seems "normal" in your context.

Your children need you to model the Heavenly Father's love for them, including guidance and discipline. They desperately need rules developed and implemented out of your love for them, as you teach them to make wise decisions. You may need the truth that those on your team or others might not share because they worry about hurting your feelings.

My style is quite direct. I would rather risk hurting your feelings now than for you to say later, "Someone should have told me!" and I did not.

Your child needs you to be the best parent you can be.

———— Section One—TCK-Specific Challenges ————

Rules and expectations may be substantially different for local children.
- Your children may have to **study a religion** in school that is contrary to yours.
- The cultural norm may be a complete lack of discipline as you try to teach your children respect for others.

See a need, meet a need.
- When you struggle, other parents either share in your struggle or did.
- Look for solutions together, then share with other parents.

— Transitions and Losses —

Life on the field generates more and different losses than a more "stable" life in one's passport country.

TCKs typically experience more transitions and losses than children who remain in their passport country or primary culture.
- Even if losses are minor, the **cumulative effect may be substantial** if they are not regularly processed.
- **Frequent moves** create additional losses.
  - Help your child understand what they will and will not see again.
  - "**Good goodbyes**" are important—for people and places.
- For those six years old and older, go through a **multi-day family debrief** after each major transition.
  - While many organizations offer these, I recommend LeRucher.org.

Regularly discuss difficulties and losses with your child.
- Give them **permission to be sad.**
- Teach them how to **grieve their losses.**
  - They will work through their grief if you process their losses with them.
- **Be honest and share your losses** as well, adjusting your story to their cognitive level.
- Lauren Well's book, *Raising Up a Generation of Healthy Third Culture Kids*, provides tools to help you help your child adapt and adjust.
  - It provides insights into challenges you might overlook (as I did!).
  - It is secular, so you will need to adapt to what Scripture teaches.

Your child may need **specific counseling for unplanned, unexpected transitions**, such as:
- **Evacuation** due to security or other concerns
- **Visa denials**, sometimes after landing with no warning.

Trauma, true trauma, may be more prevalent.
- Frontier justice may rule where you live.
- Your children may see or experience unsettling events with or without you present.

— *Travel* —

Life on the field often includes much more travel than other vocations.
- This is a great time for focused attention on your child.
  - You will remember your time together more than the movie you do not watch.
- More frequent international travel **complicates a child's sense of home.**
  - Visa runs to other countries may add confusion.
  - Retreats and conferences may impact their school rhythms.
  - Returns to passport country for weddings and deaths take longer.

- Make sure your child is well rested before beginning travel.
- When old enough, give them their own carry-on bag, and teach them how to pack it.
  - Provide age-appropriate autonomy.
  - Make sure their **headsets work** and they are used to them before travel.
  - Provide some inexpensive **new travel toys** that you will not miss if lost.
  - **Keep carry-on bags light**—they feel heavier the longer you travel.
- Children may or may not fall asleep easily.
  - Make sure you sleep whenever you can!
- Ask your peers for advice, tips, and tricks.
- Give older teens as much autonomy as they can realistically manage.
  - Teach them how to navigate travel.

— School —

Schooling decisions are more complicated in a third culture, especially in ministry.
- NGOs and embassies often provide for a private school aligned with your passport country.
- Those in other ministries may be on your own.
- Some cities or countries require all children to attend government schools where your children may be taught contrary to your beliefs.
- You will have to be especially diligent to listen and teach.
- For teens particularly, where college applications become important, an International Baccalaureate program or online program from a recognized provider in the country in which they want to attend university may be the best option.

— Home School—

Many families choose to home school where they can provide an education that will **better prepare their child for further study in their passport country.**

Models

- **Full time**—Mom and Dad share teaching, or only one teaches
- **Hybrid**—teaching is shared with other parents in your community
  - **Agree on curriculum** well in advance.
- **Online**—curriculum is internet-based, with parents overseeing the schedule
- **Private tutor**—families either hire a local tutor or someone from their passport country (or elsewhere) to teach their children as a self-supported ministry or with expenses paid by a family or shared among families

Benefits

- **Adaptable** to each child
- Can **incorporate religious instruction** aligned with parents' beliefs
- Allows **each parent to teach** their strengths
  - Frees up the other parent for ministry during school time
- **Flexible scheduling** to adapt to ministry and travel needs

Drawbacks

- It may be **illegal** in your country.
- **Fewer interactions can lead to loneliness.**
  - This may be more extreme in a cross-cultural context where so much else highlights your child's sense of being different.

Considerations

- **Adapt your work schedule** to incorporate your child's school.
- **Do not add** home-schooling **to an already-full workload.**
  - Cut out something.
  - Overfilling your day adds extra stress that leads to burnout.

When to start

- **Do not rush** a very young child.
  - **Playtime** is a valuable social and educational period for young children.

- Ensure your child has time for play after you start home-schooling.
- If you might switch to traditional school at some point, be careful you do not get your child **far ahead of their age/grade level**.
  - If your child is advanced, augment their curriculum with topics they love but might get less of in school, like art, nature, gardening, sports, dance, etc.
- **Do not hinder them**, either.
  - Our daughter started reading when she was three, not because we taught her, but because she picked it up.
  - We were not about to stop her, but did not push her.

— *Language* —

Many parents are enamored with a young child learning another language. In cross-cultural ministry or work, this may not be an enticing challenge but a cultural necessity.

- **Some language delay is common** for young children growing up bilingually.
  - Teach your child words and phrases in the local language so that they can relate on the playground.
- When your child is school-aged, a **language tutor** would be helpful for home-schooled children or if your child's school does not provide this.
- For teens, if they are to interact with locals, ensure their language instruction is geared towards their age group.
  - Learning from someone in their fifties will not provide them with the appropriate local vernacular for a teen.

— *Family Rhythms* —

If you move to a culture with dramatically different family rhythms, determine if these are the rhythms you want for your children.

Your life must look different after you have children.

- You cannot live the same lives you lived before children.
- The sacrifices you make to develop or maintain healthy family rhythms are most pronounced with very young children.
- **Take turns missing events** to preserve a young child's sleep schedule.

Young children who **follow a schedule** are better adjusted.
- If the predominant parenting in your new culture is free-flowing and anti-schedule, know that:
  - This is not unique to field life.
  - Your family's schedule may be quite different from other team members or locals.
- Put your **young children to bed a few hours earlier** than you go to bed.
  - Young children need more sleep than adults.
  - They also tend to do better with a **fixed sleep time** each night (as do adults).
  - You need the time in the evenings to **debrief your day and be a couple.**
- **Early-evening bedtime with a late-night ministry** need that requires you both requires a babysitter so that your young child can maintain their routine.
  - You might **recruit a single or couple** whose ministry is **child care and/or home-schooling** for your family or your team.
  - Do not rely on team members, especially if you are a leader.
    - Most came for ministry, not child care.
- Be sensitive to **exhaustion-based disobedience.**
  - If your schedule regularly precludes adequate time for your child to rest or eat, **you invite a disaster of your own making.**
  - Unplanned travel delays and other events will undermine your best plans.
  - Pray for the Holy Spirit to give you and your children the peace and patience you both need.

Develop **travel-friendly rhythms.**

- **Slow down.**
  - Establish sustainable rhythms that you can carry with you anywhere to help **provide stability** during periods of travel.
  - Examples include pizza night, movie night, special breakfasts, and a bedtime routine with stories.
- Read together, create holiday traditions to look forward to each year, play games that do not require a battery or power cord.

What is the **best gift for children?**
- **A healthy marriage.**
- **Husbands, court your wife!**
  - Time away from those bundles of joy is important for you and for them!
  - Find a regular babysitter—maybe the teenage child of a teammate, a ministry partner, or someone from your church.

Develop a social outlet beyond your team.
  - It is unrealistic to expect your team to meet all of your relational needs.

— Security —

Families serving on the mission field may have to think differently about security.
- Talk to the expatriates who are there with children of a similar age.
- **Understand cultural norms**—what is appropriate or not.
- **Learn the risks.**
- Explain to children, especially young children, how they may be treated as foreigners.
- Develop a "code word" (e.g., popcorn) to say if they are uncomfortable, without raising alarm or being disrespectful.

— *Team Meetings* —

Team meetings, trainings, and prayer times are **not events for most young children**.
- Team members are there to **learn, pray, or study**.
  - **Disruptions** break that flow.
  - People may not be able to hear or concentrate.
- Children allowed to interrupt learn disrespect.
- **Rotate child care** in another room, or, ideally, another house.
  - If another house, ensure at least two adults or teens watch the children.
- Hire someone to watch the children if the culture and finances allow, especially to benefit a trusted local family.

Team meals provide a teaching opportunity.
- Go through "buffet" lines with a young child to **teach them how to take small portions** to respect those behind them.
- They will learn communication patterns from you and others, how to tell interesting stories, and how to wait to speak.

— *Behavior or Actions that Warrant Further Evaluation* —

A community of other parents with children of the same age or slightly older with regular interaction plus mentors whose children are one or two life stages ahead of you will help you understand what is "developmentally normal."

Often, ministry locations are limited in the kinds of child-development services available.

Anecdote: Our son had some developmental challenges when he was quite young that were corrected through occupational therapy, which opened our eyes to the worlds of speech therapy and other sensory-motor differences. Many of these can be corrected in a relatively short time with the right medical intervention or occupational therapy.

For a complete list of developmental milestones, visit www.cdc.gov/ncbddd/actearly/milestones/index.html.

Behaviors in young children that might warrant further evaluation include:

- **Extremely late use of words**
  - Your child's language should be roughly in line with other children their age in the same context.
- **Hypersensitivity** to touch, fabrics, sounds, tastes, textures
- **Unusual physical behaviors** like walking on their toes, constant picking at their skin
- **Fixation** on future events such that they cannot focus on anything else

For late middle school, teens, and young adults, seek counsel for these and other serious behaviors.

- **Abrupt change** in moods or personality
- Withdrawal
- **Unexpected change in diet,** including the need to go to the toilet soon after eating every meal
- Cutting or other **self-harm**

Discuss any concerns with your healthcare provider.

- Do not wait for your home visit or because you are embarrassed.
- Schedule an in-person visit while you are in your passport country.
  - Do this early in your visit to provide time for additional testing or to start treatment.
  - Plan ahead, as some countries take many months to set up an appointment.
- More severe anomalies may require you to return to your passport country for a period, including indefinitely.
  - **Do not ruin your child's opportunity** for joy and thriving because your identity is tied to being a missionary or working for an NGO, etc.
  - Do not be too stubborn or prideful to get your child the help they need.

——— Section Two—Abridged Parenting Advice ———

The following is a summary of some of the top parenting advice I have read, written, learned, and taught. This is a complicated and often emotional topic, which is why this chapter has the longest list of additional resources.

You are not alone.
- **PRAY** with and for your children, but never at them.
  - Let them pray first, then support their prayers.
  - Celebrate what you cannot do that God can.
  - Teach them how to pray—at every age.
- **God chose you** to parent the child he has given you to steward for him.
- **He will prepare you**, but it is still a lot of work.
- If he called you to serve him cross-culturally, he called your child to the experience with you.
- Ask him to help you be **your child's firm foundation.**
- **Find mentors** at least one life phase ahead of you with well-behaved children.
  - Advice comes cheap.
  - Look for evidence of effective parenting in those from whom you seek advice.

— You Teach Your Child Intentionally or Unintentionally —

You never stop teaching your child. Here are some examples of intentional and unintentional teaching.

What you say or do	What it teaches
Honor the Sabbath	How to rest
Honor your spouse	How to relate well to others
Confess and repent	How to reconcile with God and others

What you say or do	What it teaches
Read Scripture and strive to reflect it in your life	God's word is where you find your source of strength and wisdom
Tell your child to tell the person at the door you are not home	Lying is acceptable
Provide snacks because children do not finish their meals	Unhealthy diet patterns and another way to manipulate you to get what they want
Allow your child to interrupt you when you are interacting with others (emergencies excepted)	How to be rude and self-centered
Respond when your child whines or yells	Whining or yelling is how you get what you want. This may also lead to worry or feelings of abandonment if there is an emergency because they have "cried wolf" too often.[9]
Jump at every demand	Impatience, that your child is the center of your universe
Invite adult children to live in your home who neither pay you nor contribute to the care and maintenance of the home	Laziness and entitlement. You deprive your child of the successes and failures they need to mature and contribute to society.

Children are smart and efficient. They do what works. Count to three before you discipline? That means more time to play. Ignore them when they whine? They stop whining. Sweet children often use their sweetness to manipulate parents and get away with disobedience.

You are your child's primary teacher. You are responsible for your child's upbringing. When you arrive at the pearly gates, do not expect dispensation for undisciplined children because you served on the field.

---

9   Hague, Michael. 1985. Aesop's Fables. New York, Holt, Rinehart, and Winston.

— *General Suggestions* —

Some parenting information is the same regardless of your situation. Learn from my mistakes and take advantage of what I have seen work well.

God does not need you.
- **Your child needs you.**
- God can raise up workers for anything he wants accomplished.
  - **Your child has one dad and one mom.**

Read *Parenting* by Paul Tripp.
- The best book on parenting principles I have read, and I have read many.

Develop and maintain a **high warmth / high discipline** parenting framework.
- **Authoritarian,** not authoritative[10]
- **Enter your child's world** at every age.
  - Learn who they are, open a door for them to share their fears and concerns, to seek your advice, and to **grow closer to you.**
  - Zig Ziglar said, "To a child, **love is spelled T-I-M-E.**"
- **Pick your battles,** but win the battles you pick!
  - Children are far more ready to obey when they know you love them unconditionally.
  - **Establish rules and consequences and hold to them.**
  - "For the Lord disciplines the one he loves, and chastises every son whom he receives." (Hebrews 12:16)
  - Say what you mean and mean what you say.
    - Inconsistency leads to uncertainty, confusion, and instability for your child.

---

[10] Conville, Nicola, "There are FOUR parenting styles but THIS one raises more successful kids," Practical Parenting, July 2, 2019, www.practicalparenting.com.au/four-parenting-stylesbut-this-one-raises-more-successful-kids.

- **Use fewer words** when you discipline.
  - ○ Save conversations for times of non-conflict, then still use fewer words.
- **Do not apologize for discipline.**
  - ○ You may need to apologize for the magnitude of the punishment, but never for the discipline itself.
- **Do not negotiate.**
  - ○ Your "yes" must be "yes," and your "no" must be "no."
  - ○ There is room for a new decision if your child brings you new information, but not if they beg or try to wear you down.
- **Do not try to conform your child to you.**
  - ○ Your goal cannot be to create a "mini me."

Do not do for your child what they can do for themselves.
- You will be amazed by your child's capabilities, which they learn by watching you.
- Give them increased responsibilities and expect more as they get older.

Dads, God has chosen you for a unique role.
- The way you parent should **prepare your child to seek the perfect Father.**
  - ○ That should terrify you, and drive you to be the best father you can be.
- Children who learn to submit to a good but flawed earthly father (and mother) are trained to submit to a perfect Heavenly Father.

Encouragement

Parenting is difficult and demanding but also the most rewarding work you will ever do. Raising your child in an unfamiliar culture, among people who look and speak and act differently than you, and whose lifestyle, morals, and religion are contrary to those you try to instill in your child, complicates your job.

You are not the only parent struggling to navigate this difficult gift in a challenging place. Connect with other parents! Read a book together, do fun things together, depend on each other for counsel, and watch each other's children to provide "date night" opportunities.

The evil one wants to isolate you. He wants you to fail. He wants your child, he wants to destroy your marriage, he wants to force you to leave the field. Be strong and courageous, and seek support in prayer.

Your Father in heaven loves your child more than you can on your best day, and he chose you to be their parent. Children are incredibly forgiving because their love for you is so great. If every day your child knows you love them through your words and actions, you will find discipline easier and your relationship deepen. Invest your time in them.

God does not need you to do his work—you get to participate.

Your child needs you.

Behold, children are a heritage from the Lord, the fruit of the womb a reward.

—Psalm 127:3

I would argue that the most important words that TCKs need to hear from their parents are these: "You are more important than our work."

—Lauren Wells,
Raising Up a Generation of Healthy Third Culture Kids

Sample Prayer

Lord, there is no more important job you give me than to raise my child to know and love you, to teach them how to behave in a way that honors you and our family, and to know we love them more than they can imagine. Help me to model imperfectly how you love them perfectly. Holy Spirit, please give me the wisdom you promise in James 1:5–8 to shepherd this child you have loaned to me.

Parenting is hard. Please help me not to make it harder. I want to raise this child you have loaned to me to become the person you want him or her to be, not the person I want them to be.

Please turn my child's heart to you and help me to guide their relationship with you.

---------- **Disclaimer** ----------

My views and opinions are my own and may or may not align with any entity with which I am now or have been affiliated. They may also not align with your sending agency, fellowship, or company.

---------- **Additional Resources** ----------

Bucknam, Robert and Gary Ezzo, *On Becoming Babywise* (sleep training)

Chandler, Lauren, *Goodbye to Goodbyes (Tales That Tell the Truth)* (Picture Book)

Dobson, James C., **The Dr. James Dobson Parenting Collection**

Doerrfeld, Cori, *The Rabbit Listened* (Picture Book)

Dumaplin, Cara, takingcarababies.com (sleep training)

Ernvik, Ulrika, *Third Culture Kids*

Haidt, Jonathan, *The Anxious Generation*

Harakal, David, *Parenting Through the Ranks*

Johnson, Helen and Christine Schelhas-Miller, *Don't Tell Me What to Do, Just Send Money*

Lantz, Matt, *A Method for Dating: Because dating happens ... and it doesn't have to be horrible* (thedatingblook.wordpress.com)

LeRucher.org (for individual and family debriefing)

Medina, Meg and Sonia Sánchez, *Evelyn Del Rey Is Moving Away* (Picture Book)

Pollock, David, Ruth E. Van Reken, et al., *Third Culture Kids*

Renée, Marci and Layken Davey, *The Boy of Many Colors* (Picture Book)

Rubio, Sarah Parker and Fátima Anaya, *Far from Home* (Picture Book)

Saunders, Sara, *Swirly* (Picture Book)

Seeker, Meg, **Strong Fathers, Strong Daughters**

Shrier, Abigail, *Bad Therapy*

Tripp, Paul David, **Parenting**

Wells, Lauren, *Raising Up a Generation of Healthy Third Culture Kids*

Wells, Lauren, *The Grief Tower*

Notes

Notes

APPENDIX

— SELF-CARE CONTACT LIST —

Based on the checklist published by Reliant Mission (reliant.org) for those they support.

For the "How connecting questions" ensure you have an email contact, messaging phone number and/or number for messaging platform (e.g., WhatsApp, Signal, etc.) and that all the contacts you have work. If the person does not respond in a timely manner (one to two days), find a new contact.

Sending Fellowship

- Who is my primary contact?
    - How often will we connect?
    - How will we connect?
- To whom will I communicate prayer requests?
    - How will we connect?
- Which pastor, elder, deacon, or other leader is assigned to me?
    - How often will we connect?
    - How will we connect?

Field Team

- Who is my supervisor?

- How will we connect? (in person/virtual)
- How often will we meet?
- Who are my other teammates?
- Who can I trust for accountability?
  - How often will we meet?
  - What is the focus of those meetings?
- Who will I trust with my location information?
- Who will trust me with theirs?
- With whom will I primarily communicate day-to-day challenges?

Personal Network
- What one or two relationships are most important to me to maintain?
  - How often will we connect?
  - How will we connect?
- Who leads my Advocacy team?
  - How often will we connect?
  - How will we connect?
- For married couples: Who are our marriage mentors?
  - How will we connect?
  - How often will we connect?
- For parents: Who are our parenting mentors?
  - How will we connect?
  - How often will we connect?

Extended Personal Support
- Who are important mentor relationship(s) in my life?
  - How will that relationship look when I am overseas?
- Do I need a mental health professional/counselor?
  - How often will we meet if so?
- Who is my primary doctor?
  - Will I have access to them overseas?
  - Is there online or phone access to doctors or nurses? What is the link?

- o How will I access any current prescriptions once overseas?
- o Who are the trusted doctors in my country?
- What are signs for myself that I may need more specialized care?
    - o To whom have I communicated those signs?

Local Support
- Who is a local friend to whom I can openly ask cultural questions?
- Who is someone with whom I could hang out on a day off?
- Who is an expat in my city with whom I might develop a friendship?
- Where is a "third space" where I can meet new people?
    - o Some place "nonthreatening" for locals and expatriates.
- Is there a theologically sound church that is safe to attend?

Personal
- What are activities I can do on the field that reduce stress or give me energy?
- In a normal ministry season, what is my day off?
    - o How will I spend it?
- What are my non-negotiable rhythms, even in a transitional season?

Sending Organization Contacts
Who can help me:
- Find member care resources?
- Help me with raising support?
- Help me with my budget or monthly spending needs?
- Answer questions about my paycheck or reimbursements?

With whom do I communicate if:
- I need to travel outside my country of ministry.
- My supervisor changes.
- I will travel for home leave/furlough.
- I would like to take a sabbatical.
- I experience a significant crisis.

- I am considering a change in my ministry partnership.
- I am unable to resolve conflict with my team or supervisor.
- I need to report misconduct.
- I am planning to exit the field.
- For any topics not listed.

GLOSSARY

Burnout

Burnout is a syndrome conceptualized as resulting from chronic workplace stress that has not been successfully managed. It is characterized by three dimensions:
1. feelings of energy depletion or exhaustion;
2. increased mental distance from one's job, or feelings of negativism or cynicism related to one's job; and
3. reduced professional efficacy.[11]

Cross-culture

Life in a culture other than your passport country or country you consider home.

Field

The generic term for places people go for ministry outside of their passport or home country.

Furlough

An extended return to one's passport or home country (generally one to twelve months) for rest, refreshment, to raise support, and to connect with supporters, or any combination thereof. Other terms include home leave and HMA (Home Ministry Assignment).

---

[11] From the World Health Organization: www.who.int/news/item/28-05-2019-burn-out-an-occupational-phenomenon-international-classification-of-diseases

Go bag

A small bag packed with clothing, travel documents, cash, and other required items that one can grab quickly in case of an urgent evacuation stored generally in one's home.

Goer

Another word for missionary. The idea is that some go (goers) and some send (senders). This is most often referenced by John Piper in his quote, "Go, send, or disobey." (Note: "goer", "cross-cultural worker", and related terms, are often used in place of the word "missionary" as it has accumulated baggage, partly due to association with "colonialism," which has fallen out of vogue.)

Good goodbye

When leaving a home, passport, or host country, establishing closure with people, places, and things. See RAFT below.

HMA (Home Ministry Assignment)

An extended return to one's passport or home country (generally one to twelve months) for rest, refreshment, to raise support, and to connect with supporters, or any combination thereof. Other terms include furlough and home leave.

Home leave

An extended return to one's passport or home country (generally one to twelve months) for rest, refreshment, to raise support, and to connect with supporters, or any combination thereof. Other terms include furlough and HMA (Home Ministry Assignment).

Mobilizer

A person, generally in one's home or passport country, who prepares a missionary for deployment.

MOU

Memorandum of Understanding—an agreement which is not legally binding between an individual and a team, or between a team and an organization, or any combination thereof. This sets out norms and expectations to provide clarity and avoid misunderstandings. See the "Contracting" chapter in Section 2 for a more thorough description.

NGO

Non-Governmental Organization—generally charitable organizations which vary in size from a few individuals to the International Committee of the Red Cross and Red Crescent.

Passport country

Used in lieu of "home country," as many cross-cultural workers consider their host country "home." Some also use the phrase "primary culture."

Platform

The official reason a cross-cultural worker is in a host country, which could be working for a corporation or NGO, building a business, coaching teams, language study, etc.

RAFT

Process for "good goodbyes" from the book *Third Culture Kids* by David Pollock, et al. See the "Leaving" chapter for additional details.

Reverse culture shock

"Reverse culture shock is experienced when returning to a place that one expects to be home but actually is no longer." - Dean Foster, founder and president of DFA Intercultural Global Solutions

Scope creep

The process of increasing workload little by little until it is untenable or promotes burnout. It typically results from either "temporary" needs that become permanent or redistributing workload as people leave a team or organization without adjusting the existing tasks or schedule.

Secondment

Pronounced /sɪˈkɒn(d)m(ə)nt/ - The result of an individual moving their operational responsibilities to one organization while their funding and financial management is through a different organization. This facilitates people joining new teams as new opportunities are presented without the need to change their "employer" and supporters changing their payment location.

Sender

Someone who supports a goer in prayer and/or financially. The idea is that some go (goers) and some send (senders). This is most often referenced by John Piper in his quote, "Go, send, or disobey."

TCK

Third-Culture Kid—a child who grows up in a culture different from the one in which his or her parents grew up, coined by American sociologist Ruth Useem (1915-2003).

Visa run

Depending on one's visa type, many countries require non-citizens to leave the country regularly. Because these are typically quick trips of a weekend or less to a nearby country, they have picked up the phrase "visa run."

CONSOLIDATED RESOURCE LIST

Books, blogs, courses, and podcasts for further study

The beginning of wisdom is this: Get wisdom, and whatever you get, get insight.
—Proverbs 4:7

The first priority of my life is to be holy, and the second goal of my life is to be a scholar.
—John Wesley

I have read every book on this list (except the picture books, which were recommended by a trusted mom of young children). Podcasts I have listened to enough to support them. (I am more of a reader than a listener.) There are myriad other resources, many quite good, but as I have not read or listened to them, I will not recommend them.

Moving to a new does country not require a PhD., but does require the desire to learn and study. You will find different resources helpful at different times, but please do not think that I recommend you read them all. I quote very few of these because the information is common and aligned with what I had already written, only the packaging differs.

The ones I most recommend are in bold, and I noted those specific to marriage or parenting, which may not be obvious from the titles.

Bibliography

Allberry, Sam, *7 Myths About Singleness*. Crossway, 2019.

Alma, Carissa, **Thriving in Cross-Cultural Ministry**. Pavilion Books, 2011.

Bell, Bradley, Mike Easton, et al., *The Sending Church Applied*. The Upstream Collective, 2024.

Bradley, Zach, et al., *Receiving Sent Ones During Reentry: The Challenges of Returning "Home" and How Churches Can Help*. The Upstream Collective, 2017.

Bucknam, Robert and Ezzo, Gary, *On Becoming Babywise: Giving Your Infant the Gift of Nighttime Sleep*. Parent-Wise Solutions, Inc., 2020. (Parenting)

Chandler, Lauren, *Goodbye to Goodbyes (Tales That Tell the Truth)*. The Good Book Company, 2019. (Picture Book)

Chaplin, Melissa, *Returning Well: Your Guide to Thriving Back "Home" after Serving Cross-Culturally*. Newton Publishers, 2015.

Coleman, Robert E., *The Master Plan of Evangelism*. Revellbooks, 2010.

Corbett, Steve and Brian Fikkert, *When Helping Hurts: How to Alleviate Poverty Without Hurting the Poor ... and Yourself*. Moody Publishers, 2014.

Corbett, Steve, Brian Fikkert, and Katie Casselberry, **Helping Without Hurting in Church Benevolence**: *A Practical Guide to Walking with Low-Income People*. Moody Publishers, 2014.

Dobson, James C., **The Dr. James Dobson Parenting Collection** (Includes *The New Dare to Discipline*, *The New Strong-Willed Child*, and *Parenting Isn't for Cowards*). Tyndale Momentum, 2011. (Parenting)

Doerrfeld, Cori, *The Rabbit Listened*. Dial Books, 2018. (Picture Book)

Druckerman, Pamela, *Bringing Up Bébé: One American Mother Discovers the Wisdom of French Parenting*. Penguin Books, 2014. (See important caveat in the Parenting chapter.)

Eggerichs, Dr. Emerson, **Love and Respect**: *The Love She Most Desires; The Respect He Desperately Needs*. Thomas Nelson, 2004. (Mariage)

Eenigenburg, Sue and Eva Burkholder, *Grit to Stay Grace to Go: Staying Well in Cross-Cultural Ministry*. William Carey Publishing, 2023.

Ernvik, Ulrika, *Third Culture Kids: A Gift to Care For*. Familjagladje, 2019. (Parenting)

Frazier, David, **Mission Smart:** *15 Critical Questions To Ask Before Launching Overseas.* CreateSpace Independent Publishing Platform, 2013.

Grudem, Wayne, **Systematic Theology, Second Edition:** *An Introduction to Biblical Doctrine.* Zondervan Academic, 2020.

Hale, Thomas, *On Being a Missionary (Abridged):An Introduction to Cross-Cultural Life and Ministry.* William Carey Library Publishers, 2012.

Haidt, Jonathan, *The Anxious Generation: How the Great Rewiring of Childhood Is Causing an Epidemic of Mental Illness.* Penguin Press, 2024. (Parenting)

Harakal, David, **Parenting Through the Ranks:** *How to Raise Successful Scouts.* Falcon Guides, 2024. (Parenting) (I imagine I should recommend my own book. Though written for Scouts, the information is good for any parent.)

Henderson, John, *Catching Foxes: A Gospel-Guided Journey to Marriage.* P&R Publishing, 2018. (Marriage)

Johnson, Helen and Christine Schelhas-Miller, *Don't Tell Me What to Do, Just Send Money: The Essential Parenting Guide to the College Years.* Golden Guides from St. Martin's Press, 2011. (Parenting)

Kruger, Michael J., *Bully Pulpit: Confronting the Problem of Spiritual Abuse in the Church.* Zondervan, 2022.

Lanier, Sarah, **Foreign to Familiar, 2nd Edition:** *A Guide to Understanding Hot- and Cold-Climate Cultures.* McDougal Publishing Company, 2022.

Lantz, Matt, *A Method for Dating: Because dating happens … and it doesn't have to be horrible.* (thedatingblook.wordpress.com)

McKie, Rusty, *Sabbaticals: "How-To" Take a Break from Ministry before Ministry Breaks You.* Sojourn Network, 2018.

McNabb, Dr. Bob, *Spiritual Multiplication in the Real World: Why Some Disciple-Makers Reproduce when Others Fail.* Multiplication Press, 2013.

Medina, Meg and Sonia Sanchez, *Evelyn Del Rey Is Moving Away.* Candlewick, 2023. (Picture Book)

Piper, John, *Let the Nations Be Glad!: The Supremacy of God in Missions.* Baker Academic, 2022.

Pollock, David, Ruth E. Van Reken, et al., *Third Culture Kids 3rd Edition: Growing Up Among Worlds.* Nicholas Brealey, 2017. (Parenting)

Reid, Dr. Alvin L. and Malcolm McDow, et al., *Firefall 2.0: How God Has Shaped History Through Revivals.* CreateSpace Independent Publishing Platform, 2014.

Reju, Deepak, *Pornography: Fighting for Purity (31-Day Devotionals for Life).* P&R Publishing, 2018.

Reju, Deepak and Jonathan Holmes, *Rescue Plan: Charting a Course to Restore Prisoners of Pornography.* P&R Publishing, 2021.

Reju, Deepak and Jonathan Holmes, *Rescue Skills: Essential Skills for Restoring the Sexually Broken.* P&R Publishing, 2021.

Renée, Marci and Layken Davey, *The Boy of Many Colors (Pierre's World Traveling Adventures).* The Cultural Story-Weaver, 2021. (Picture Book)

Ripkin, Nik, *The Insanity of God: A True Story of Faith Resurrected.* B&H Books, 2014.

Rubio, Sarah Parker and Fátima Anaya, *Far from Home: A Story of Loss, Refuge, and Hope.* Tyndale Kids, 2019. (Picture Book)

Saunders, Sara, *Swirly.* Review & Herald Publishing Association, 2012. (Picture Book)

Seeker, Meg, **Strong Fathers, Strong Daughters:** *10 Secrets Every Father Should Know.* Regnery, 2017. (Parenting)

Shadrach, Steve and Scott Morton, *The God Ask: A Fresh, Biblical Approach to Personal Support Raising.* CMM Press, 2013.

Shaw, Joey, *All Authority: How the Authority of Jesus Upholds the Great Commission.* B&H Publishing Group, 2016.

Shrier, Abigail, *Bad Therapy: Why the Kids Aren't Growing Up.* Sentinel, 2024. (Parenting)

Taylor, Dr. and Mrs. Howard, **Hudson Taylor's Spiritual Secret.** Moody Publishers, 2009.

Tripp, Paul David, **Parenting:** *14 Gospel Principles That Can Radically Change Your Family.* Crossway, 2024. (Parenting)

Wells, Lauren, *Raising Up a Generation of Healthy Third Culture Kids: A Practical Guide to Preventive Care.* Independently Published, 2020. (Parenting)

Wells, Lauren, *The Grief Tower: A Practical Guide to Processing Grief with Third Culture Kids.* Independently Published, 2021. (Parenting)

Weyeneth, Sandy, *Writing Exceptional Missionary Newsletters: Essentials for Writing, Producing, and Sending Newsletters that Motivate Readers.* William Carey Library, 2013.

Winter, Ralph D. and Steven C. Hawthorne, *Perspectives on the World Christian Movement: A Reader*. William Carey Library Publishers, 2009.

Young, Amy, *Getting Started: Making the Most of Your First Year in Cross-Cultural Service*. Independently Published, 2019.

Young, Amy, *Looming Transitions: Starting and Finishing Well in Cross-Cultural Service*. CreateSpace Independent Publishing Platform, 2021.

Young, Amy, *Enjoying Newsletters: How to Write Christian Communications People Want to Read*. Independently Published, 2019.

Zerub, Caleb, *Nations Prep Handbook*. Independently Published, 2022.

Podcasts/Websites

Antioch Waco, *Resiliency* podcast

Dumaplin, Cara, takingcarababies.com (Parenting—infant sleep training)

Grudem, Wayne, *Systematic Theology* teaching website

Sanctuary Inn, *The Innkeepers* podcast

Courses/Programs

Debriefing—LeRucher.org (for individual and family)

Finance and Investments—Ramsey, Dave, "Financial Peace University," www.ramseysolutions.com/ramseyplus/financial-peace

Leading—*Grace Academy Leadership Lab* www.grace.northpass.com

Marriage—*Re|engage*—reengage.org

Marriage—*A Weekend to Remember* (U.S.)—familylife.com/weekend-to-remember/

Parenting—*Getting to the Heart of Parenting*—store.paultripp.com/collections/getting-to-the-heart-of-parenting

Parenting—*Christ-Centered Parenting* by Russell D. Moore and Phillip Bethancourt (Amazon)

Parenting—www.tcktraining.com/for-parents

Prayer—*Hour of Prayer* by The Austin Stone—*austinstone.org/videos/hour-of-prayer*